Web Application Pentesting

Pentesting

James Relington

DEDICATION

To those who tirelessly safeguard digital systems, ensuring security
and trust in an ever-evolving digital world—this book is dedicated to
you. Your commitment to protecting access, enforcing governance,
and navigating the complexities cybersecurity is invaluable. May this
work serve as a guide and inspiration in your ongoing efforts to create
a more secure and compliant future.

AKNOWLEDGEMENTS

I extend my deepest gratitude to everyone who contributed to the creation of this book. To my colleagues and mentors in the field of identity governance, your insights and expertise have been invaluable. To my friends and family, your unwavering support and encouragement have made this journey possible. To the professionals and innovators dedicated to securing digital identities, your work continues to inspire and shape the future of cybersecurity. This book is a reflection of collective knowledge, and I am grateful to all who have played a role in its development.

Introduction to Web Application Security

Web application security is a fundamental aspect of modern cybersecurity, ensuring that the services and data hosted on the web remain protected against a wide range of malicious activities. In recent years, as more organizations migrate critical business functions online, the importance of securing web applications has grown exponentially. This chapter explores the core concepts of web application security, examining the types of threats that exist and the principles that underpin effective defenses.

A web application is essentially a client-server software application that runs on a web server and is accessed through a web browser. This accessibility is both a strength and a vulnerability. While it allows businesses to reach users across the globe with ease, it also exposes applications to an array of threats that target their underlying infrastructure, logic, and data. Attackers often exploit weaknesses in code, design, or configuration to compromise these systems, aiming to gain unauthorized access, manipulate data, or disrupt services.

Understanding the nature of these threats is key to building a secure web application. Threats come in many forms: targeted attacks from skilled adversaries, automated scans by malicious bots, or even accidental exposure due to misconfigurations. Common vulnerabilities, such as cross-site scripting (XSS), SQL injection, and insecure direct object references (IDOR), illustrate how seemingly minor flaws in an application's logic or data handling can lead to significant breaches. Each of these vulnerabilities represents a different angle of attack, making it crucial for developers, administrators, and security teams to adopt a multi-layered defense approach.

One of the core principles in web application security is the concept of defense in depth. Instead of relying on a single security measure, this approach involves deploying multiple, overlapping controls to protect against various attack vectors. For instance, developers might implement input validation to prevent malicious data from being processed, while administrators enforce robust authentication measures to ensure only authorized users can access sensitive resources. At the same time, monitoring tools can detect unusual patterns of behavior, alerting security teams to potential intrusions before significant damage is done.

Another essential principle is the concept of least privilege. By restricting users, services, and applications to only the permissions they absolutely need, organizations can limit the potential impact of a compromise. If an attacker gains access to a low-privilege user account, for example, they are less likely to move laterally through the system or access sensitive data. Applying least privilege requires careful planning, frequent reviews of access rights, and consistent enforcement through both technical controls and organizational policies.

Web application security also involves a strong emphasis on secure coding practices. Developers need to be aware of the common pitfalls that lead to vulnerabilities and should follow established guidelines, such as those outlined by the Open Web Application Security Project (OWASP). These guidelines help ensure that input validation, proper error handling, and secure authentication methods are all integrated into the application from the earliest stages of development. By addressing security issues during the coding phase, organizations can significantly reduce the likelihood of vulnerabilities making it into production.

Regular testing is another cornerstone of web application security. This includes automated scans using tools that check for known vulnerabilities, as well as manual testing by skilled security professionals who can identify more complex issues. Penetration testing, in particular, helps organizations simulate real-world attacks, providing a clearer understanding of how an application's defenses hold up under pressure. This type of testing not only uncovers vulnerabilities but also highlights weaknesses in the overall security posture, prompting necessary improvements.

Beyond technical measures, fostering a security-aware culture within an organization is critical. This means ensuring that everyone involved in the application lifecycle—developers, testers, administrators, and even management—understands the importance of security and their role in maintaining it. Security training, regular updates on emerging threats, and clear communication channels for reporting potential issues all contribute to a more robust defense.

The landscape of web application security is constantly evolving. New technologies, frameworks, and methodologies emerge regularly, introducing both new opportunities and new risks. Staying ahead of these changes requires a commitment to continuous learning, vigilance, and the willingness to adapt. As organizations grow and their web applications become more complex, the need for comprehensive, well-maintained security strategies becomes even more evident.

By integrating the core principles of web application security into every stage of the development and deployment process, businesses can not only protect their data and users but also build trust and maintain their reputation in an increasingly digital world. In the following chapters, we'll delve deeper into the specific vulnerabilities and strategies that define the field, providing practical guidance and actionable insights to help secure modern web applications.

Common Vulnerabilities in Web Applications

Web applications are a critical part of the modern digital ecosystem, but their complexity also makes them vulnerable to a wide range of security threats. Attackers constantly search for weaknesses in web applications, exploiting them to gain unauthorized access, manipulate data, or disrupt services. Understanding these vulnerabilities is essential for developers, security professionals, and organizations aiming to protect their applications from cyber threats. Many of the most common vulnerabilities have been well-documented by security organizations such as the Open Web Application Security Project (OWASP), yet they continue to pose significant risks due to poor coding practices, misconfigurations, and insufficient security awareness.

One of the most prevalent vulnerabilities in web applications is SQL injection. This attack occurs when an application improperly handles user input, allowing an attacker to manipulate database queries. By inserting malicious SQL statements into an input field, an attacker can retrieve, modify, or even delete data from a database. In some cases, SQL injection can be used to escalate privileges or execute system commands, potentially leading to full server compromise. Despite being a well-known issue, SQL injection remains a significant threat because many applications still fail to implement proper input validation and use parameterized queries to mitigate the risk.

Cross-site scripting (XSS) is another widespread vulnerability that affects web applications. This attack allows an attacker to inject malicious scripts into a webpage viewed by other users. When executed, these scripts can steal sensitive information such as cookies, session tokens, or login credentials. XSS vulnerabilities typically arise when user-generated content is not properly sanitized before being rendered in the browser. There are three main types of XSS attacks: stored, reflected, and DOM-based. Stored XSS is particularly dangerous because the malicious script is permanently stored on the server and delivered to users whenever they access the affected page. Proper encoding and input validation techniques can help mitigate the risk of XSS attacks.

Cross-site request forgery (CSRF) is another serious vulnerability that exploits the trust a web application has in an authenticated user. In a CSRF attack, an attacker tricks a user into performing unintended actions on a website where they are already authenticated. For example, a malicious link or script could force a victim to transfer money, change their email address, or modify account settings without their knowledge. CSRF attacks are particularly dangerous when combined with session hijacking techniques. To defend against CSRF, applications should implement anti-CSRF tokens, enforce strict referrer policies, and require user re-authentication for sensitive actions.

Broken authentication and session management can also expose web applications to significant risks. If authentication mechanisms are not properly implemented, attackers may be able to bypass login procedures, hijack user sessions, or exploit weak password policies. Common issues include insecure password storage, improper session expiration, and the use of predictable session tokens. Multi-factor authentication (MFA) and secure session handling practices can help mitigate these risks. Developers should also ensure that session cookies are properly configured with the Secure and HttpOnly flags to reduce the risk of session hijacking.

Insecure direct object references (IDOR) represent another major threat to web applications. This vulnerability occurs when an application exposes internal object references, such as database record identifiers, in a way that allows unauthorized users to access or manipulate resources they should not have access to. For example, if a URL contains a user ID parameter that can be incremented to view another user's account details, an attacker can easily exploit this flaw. Implementing proper access controls and ensuring authorization checks are performed at every level of an application can prevent IDOR attacks.

Security misconfigurations are a frequent source of vulnerabilities in web applications. Many applications are deployed with default credentials, unnecessary services, or overly permissive settings that attackers can exploit. Common misconfigurations include exposing sensitive directories, displaying verbose error messages, and failing to apply security patches. Organizations must follow secure deployment practices, regularly audit configurations, and disable features that are not needed.

The use of vulnerable third-party components is another critical issue. Web applications often rely on open-source libraries and frameworks to function efficiently, but these components can introduce security flaws if they are not regularly updated. Attackers frequently target known vulnerabilities in outdated libraries, leading to exploits such as remote code execution and privilege escalation. Organizations must track dependencies, monitor vulnerability databases, and apply security patches in a timely manner to reduce the risk posed by outdated components.

Improper input validation remains one of the most fundamental security flaws in web applications. Many vulnerabilities, including SQL injection, XSS, and command injection, stem from inadequate input validation. Applications should treat all user input as untrusted and validate it against strict rules. Implementing a positive security model, where only explicitly allowed inputs are accepted, can significantly reduce the attack surface.

Cryptographic failures, previously known as "sensitive data exposure" in earlier OWASP Top Ten lists, continue to affect web applications. Weak encryption, improper key management, and reliance on outdated cryptographic algorithms can expose sensitive information to attackers. Web applications handling user credentials, payment data, or personal information must use strong encryption protocols, such as TLS 1.2 or later, and follow best practices for key storage and management.

Another serious vulnerability is XML External Entity (XXE) processing. This occurs when applications parse XML input without proper validation, allowing attackers to exploit XML parsers to read local files, conduct denial-of-service attacks, or interact with internal systems. Disabling external entity processing in XML parsers is a critical step in mitigating this risk.

Understanding and mitigating these vulnerabilities is essential for building secure web applications. Developers and security professionals must adopt a proactive approach, integrating security measures throughout the software development lifecycle. Regular security assessments, code reviews, and penetration testing can help identify and address vulnerabilities before they can be exploited. As web application security continues to evolve, staying informed about emerging threats and best practices is crucial for maintaining a strong security posture.

Understanding the HTTP Protocol

The Hypertext Transfer Protocol (HTTP) is the foundation of communication on the web. It defines how clients, such as web browsers, interact with servers to request and receive content. Understanding how HTTP works is essential for web application security, as many vulnerabilities arise from improper implementation or misconfigurations of this protocol. By grasping its mechanisms, developers and security professionals can better protect applications from potential threats.

HTTP is a stateless, request-response protocol, meaning that each request from a client is independent and does not retain information about previous requests. This simplicity makes HTTP efficient but also introduces challenges when maintaining user sessions, leading to the need for mechanisms like cookies and authentication tokens. A typical HTTP transaction involves a client sending a request to a server and the server responding with the requested resource or an error message. These interactions are governed by HTTP methods, headers, and status codes.

HTTP methods define the intended action of a request. The most commonly used methods are GET and POST. GET is used to retrieve information from a server, often without modifying data. POST, on the other hand, is used to send data to a server, such as form submissions or file uploads. Other methods include PUT, which updates or replaces a resource, DELETE, which removes a resource, and PATCH, which applies partial modifications to a resource. Improper handling of these methods can lead to security vulnerabilities, such as allowing unauthorized users to perform destructive actions.

HTTP headers provide additional information about a request or response. They include general headers, request headers, response headers, and entity headers. Request headers, such as User-Agent, inform the server about the client's browser and operating system. Response headers, like Server, disclose details about the web server, sometimes unintentionally revealing information that attackers can use. Security-related headers, such as Content-Security-Policy and X-Frame-Options, help mitigate threats like cross-site scripting (XSS) and clickjacking. Configuring headers properly is a critical aspect of securing web applications.

HTTP status codes indicate the outcome of a request. They are grouped into five categories: informational (1xx), successful (2xx), redirection (3xx), client errors (4xx), and server errors (5xx). A 200 OK response indicates that a request was successful, while 404 Not Found means the requested resource does not exist. Client errors, such as 403 Forbidden, indicate that access is denied due to insufficient permissions. Server errors, like 500 Internal Server Error, suggest a problem on the server side. Understanding these codes helps diagnose issues and improve application security.

The evolution of HTTP has led to multiple versions of the protocol, each addressing limitations of its predecessors. HTTP/1.1, introduced in 1997, remains widely used and supports persistent connections, reducing the overhead of establishing new connections for each request. However, HTTP/1.1 suffers from performance issues like head-of-line blocking, where a slow request can delay others. To overcome these limitations, HTTP/2 was developed, introducing multiplexing, which allows multiple requests to be sent simultaneously over a single connection. HTTP/2 also compresses headers to reduce data transfer size, improving performance. The latest version, HTTP/3, builds on these improvements by using QUIC, a transport protocol designed to reduce latency and enhance security.

Security is a major concern in HTTP communication, especially since early versions transmitted data in plaintext, making it vulnerable to interception. To address this, HTTPS (Hypertext Transfer Protocol Secure) was introduced, encrypting HTTP traffic using Transport Layer Security (TLS). HTTPS protects against man-in-the-middle attacks, ensuring data integrity and confidentiality. Most modern websites enforce HTTPS to protect user credentials, financial transactions, and other sensitive data.

Even with HTTPS, misconfigurations can expose applications to risks. For example, improper certificate management can lead to expired or self-signed certificates, triggering security warnings in browsers. Mixed content issues arise when a secure HTTPS page loads insecure HTTP resources, potentially allowing attackers to manipulate content. Implementing HTTP Strict Transport Security (HSTS) helps mitigate these risks by enforcing HTTPS-only connections.

Understanding HTTP's role in web application security extends beyond encryption. Many attacks, such as SQL injection and cross-site scripting, exploit how HTTP handles user input. Attackers often manipulate parameters in HTTP requests to execute unauthorized commands or retrieve sensitive data. Web developers and security professionals must validate and sanitize user input to prevent these threats.

Session management is another critical aspect of HTTP security. Since HTTP is stateless, web applications use cookies and tokens to track user sessions. Secure cookies should be marked with the HttpOnly and Secure flags to prevent client-side access and enforce HTTPS transmission. Improper session management can lead to session hijacking, where attackers steal session tokens to impersonate users. Implementing secure authentication and session expiration mechanisms helps mitigate these risks.

The HTTP protocol continues to evolve, adapting to new security challenges and performance demands. Understanding its structure, methods, headers, and security implications is essential for building and securing modern web applications. By implementing best practices and staying informed about emerging threats, developers and security professionals can reduce vulnerabilities and create safer online experiences.

Authentication and Session Management

Authentication and session management are critical components of web application security, ensuring that users are properly identified and their interactions are securely maintained throughout a session. These mechanisms form the backbone of user access control, preventing unauthorized access to sensitive resources. Poorly implemented authentication and session management can lead to severe security vulnerabilities, exposing applications to threats such as session hijacking, credential theft, and privilege escalation.

Authentication is the process of verifying a user's identity before granting access to a system. The most common method is password-based authentication, where users enter a username and password combination. However, passwords alone are often insufficient due to weak user-selected passwords, reuse across multiple platforms, and susceptibility to brute force attacks. To mitigate these risks, organizations implement stronger authentication mechanisms such as multi-factor authentication (MFA), which requires users to provide additional verification factors like one-time passcodes (OTP) or biometric data. Properly implemented MFA significantly enhances security by making it more difficult for attackers to gain unauthorized access, even if they obtain a user's password.

Secure password management is another crucial aspect of authentication. Storing passwords in plaintext is a fundamental mistake that can lead to massive data breaches. Instead, passwords should be hashed using strong cryptographic algorithms like bcrypt, Argon2, or PBKDF2, along with a unique salt for each password. This ensures that even if an attacker gains access to a password database, recovering the original passwords remains computationally infeasible. Additionally, enforcing password complexity requirements and periodic password rotation policies further strengthens security, though modern best practices suggest prioritizing the use of MFA over frequent password changes.

Session management is equally important, as it governs how user sessions are created, maintained, and terminated. Web applications typically use session tokens or cookies to keep track of authenticated users. A session begins when a user successfully logs in, and the server generates a unique token that is sent to the client and stored in a cookie. This token is then included in subsequent requests to maintain the user's authenticated state without requiring them to log in repeatedly.

A common vulnerability in session management is session fixation, where an attacker forces a victim to use a pre-defined session ID, allowing the attacker to hijack the session once the victim logs in. To prevent this, applications should generate a new session ID upon login and use secure session token generation mechanisms. Another major risk is session hijacking, where an attacker intercepts a user's session token, often through network sniffing, cross-site scripting (XSS), or man-in-the-middle attacks. Encrypting communication with TLS, setting cookies with the HttpOnly and Secure flags, and implementing short session timeouts help mitigate these threats.

Proper session expiration policies are essential for reducing the risk of unauthorized access. Idle session timeouts should be enforced to automatically log out inactive users after a set period. Additionally, absolute session timeouts can prevent long-lived sessions from being exploited by attackers. Logout functionality must be implemented correctly to ensure that session tokens are invalidated on the server side rather than simply being removed from the client's browser.

Another critical aspect of session security is protection against cross-site request forgery (CSRF) attacks. CSRF occurs when an attacker tricks a user into executing unauthorized actions on a web application where they are already authenticated. Implementing anti-CSRF tokens and enforcing SameSite cookie attributes help prevent attackers from exploiting a user's authenticated session to perform malicious actions.

Single sign-on (SSO) solutions enhance authentication and session management by allowing users to log in once and gain access to multiple applications without re-entering credentials. SSO implementations often rely on industry standards such as OAuth 2.0, OpenID Connect, and SAML. While SSO improves user experience and reduces password fatigue, it also introduces risks if the identity provider is compromised. Organizations must ensure that their SSO solutions are securely configured, enforce MFA, and monitor authentication activity for signs of misuse.

Authentication and session management are constantly evolving to address emerging threats. New technologies such as passwordless authentication, which leverages public-key cryptography and biometrics, are gaining traction as more secure alternatives to traditional passwords. As web applications become more complex and attackers develop new techniques, maintaining robust authentication and session management practices remains a top priority for ensuring security and protecting user data.

Exploring Input Validation and Sanitization

Input validation and sanitization are fundamental aspects of web application security, designed to prevent malicious input from compromising the integrity, functionality, and security of an application. Web applications interact with user-provided data through various means, including form submissions, API requests, URL parameters, and file uploads. If this input is not properly validated and sanitized, attackers can exploit vulnerabilities to manipulate application behavior, access unauthorized data, or execute arbitrary commands on the server.

Input validation is the process of ensuring that incoming data conforms to expected formats and values before it is processed by the application. This step is critical for preventing common vulnerabilities such as SQL injection, cross-site scripting (XSS), and command injection. Effective input validation follows a whitelist approach, where only explicitly allowed values are accepted, rather than a blacklist approach that attempts to filter out known bad inputs. For instance, if a web application expects a phone number, it should only accept numerical values within a predefined length range rather than attempting to strip out non-numeric characters from any input.

There are different types of validation, including client-side and server-side validation. Client-side validation is implemented using JavaScript or HTML5 constraints and provides immediate feedback to users, improving user experience. However, it is not a security measure since attackers can bypass it by disabling JavaScript or manipulating requests manually. Server-side validation is more robust as it ensures that data is properly checked before being processed or stored. Without proper server-side validation, an application remains vulnerable to injection attacks and other forms of input-based exploitation.

Sanitization is the process of cleaning or transforming user input to remove or neutralize potentially harmful content. Unlike validation, which rejects bad input, sanitization modifies the input to ensure it is safe to process. This is particularly important for preventing cross-site scripting (XSS) attacks, where malicious scripts are injected into web pages viewed by other users. By escaping or encoding special characters such as <, >, and &, applications can prevent these scripts from executing in the browser. HTML sanitization libraries and frameworks provide automated ways to safely process user-generated content without stripping useful formatting.

One of the key challenges in input validation and sanitization is finding the right balance between security and functionality. Overly restrictive validation may hinder legitimate users by rejecting valid inputs, while inadequate sanitization can leave applications vulnerable to attacks. Developers need to tailor validation rules based on the expected input context and apply appropriate sanitization methods based on how the data will be used. For example, an input field accepting usernames should have character limits and allow only alphanumeric characters, whereas an input field for user-generated comments may require HTML sanitization to allow safe formatting.

Different types of input require different validation and sanitization techniques. Numeric fields should be constrained to expected ranges and data types, date fields should follow standard formats, and file uploads should be restricted by type, size, and content inspection. When handling email input, regular expressions can be used to enforce correct formatting, but additional verification, such as domain validation and confirmation emails, may be necessary to ensure authenticity. Similarly, URL inputs should be validated to prevent open redirect vulnerabilities and potential phishing attempts.

Web applications should also be cautious about handling user-generated content stored in databases or displayed dynamically. Stored XSS attacks occur when malicious scripts are saved in a database and later executed when retrieved and displayed on a webpage. Proper output encoding should be applied before rendering content in HTML, JavaScript, or other execution contexts. Security libraries such as OWASP's AntiSamy and HTMLPurifier provide mechanisms to safely filter user input while preserving necessary formatting.

Another critical aspect of input validation is preventing command injection and SQL injection attacks. Command injection occurs when untrusted input is directly passed to system commands or shell scripts, allowing attackers to execute arbitrary commands on the server. SQL injection, one of the most notorious vulnerabilities, exploits improper handling of user input in database queries. Using prepared statements and parameterized queries is the most effective way to mitigate these risks. Instead of concatenating user input directly into SQL queries, applications should bind input parameters to predefined query structures, preventing malicious payloads from altering the intended query logic.

Security mechanisms should be consistently applied across all application entry points, including web forms, API endpoints, and third-party integrations. Attackers often probe different vectors to find unprotected input fields, making it essential to apply validation and sanitization uniformly. Automated security testing tools can help identify weak spots in input handling, and regular code reviews can reinforce secure coding practices.

While input validation and sanitization are powerful defenses, they should be complemented by additional security measures. Web application firewalls (WAFs) can provide an extra layer of protection by detecting and blocking suspicious input patterns before they reach the application. Logging and monitoring mechanisms can help detect unusual input attempts, allowing security teams to respond proactively to emerging threats. By adopting a comprehensive approach to input handling, developers can minimize the risk of input-based attacks and ensure a more secure user experience.

Cross-Site Scripting (XSS) Techniques

Cross-Site Scripting (XSS) is one of the most common and dangerous vulnerabilities affecting web applications. It allows attackers to inject malicious scripts into otherwise benign and trusted websites, compromising user data, stealing credentials, or manipulating website behavior. XSS attacks exploit weaknesses in how applications handle user input and dynamically generate content. Despite being well-known and documented, XSS remains a prevalent threat due to improper input validation and output encoding.

XSS vulnerabilities arise when web applications accept user input and reflect it back to users without proper sanitization. Attackers craft malicious payloads that execute JavaScript in the victim's browser, gaining control over session cookies, executing unauthorized actions, or redirecting users to phishing sites. The impact of XSS can range from minor annoyances, such as defacing web pages, to severe security breaches involving data theft and account takeovers. Understanding the different types of XSS attacks is essential for implementing effective countermeasures.

There are three main types of XSS attacks: stored, reflected, and DOM-based. Stored XSS, also known as persistent XSS, occurs when malicious scripts are permanently saved on a web server and served to users who access the affected page. This often happens in forums, comment sections, or user profile fields where input is stored in a database and later displayed without proper sanitization. Because stored XSS exploits persist on the server, they pose a high risk, especially if attackers target administrative accounts.

Reflected XSS occurs when user input is immediately included in a web response without being stored on the server. This attack relies on tricking victims into clicking a malicious link containing a script payload embedded in a URL parameter. When the request is processed, the vulnerable application reflects the malicious script in the response, causing the victim's browser to execute it. Since reflected XSS requires user interaction, attackers often distribute malicious links through phishing emails, social media, or forum posts.

DOM-based XSS differs from stored and reflected XSS in that the vulnerability resides entirely within client-side JavaScript rather than the server. In a DOM-based XSS attack, malicious scripts manipulate the Document Object Model (DOM) of a webpage, often modifying input fields, URL fragments, or JavaScript variables. This type of attack bypasses traditional server-side input validation techniques since the malicious payload is executed directly in the victim's browser. Client-side frameworks, such as React or Angular, mitigate some DOM-based XSS risks by enforcing strict data-binding mechanisms, but improper handling of user input can still introduce vulnerabilities.

To defend against XSS, developers must implement a combination of input validation, output encoding, and security headers. Input validation ensures that user-submitted data conforms to expected formats and does not contain potentially dangerous characters. However, input validation alone is not sufficient, as some XSS payloads can bypass basic filtering techniques. Output encoding is the most effective countermeasure, ensuring that user input is properly escaped before being rendered in HTML, JavaScript, or CSS. For example, encoding special characters like <, >, and & prevents them from being interpreted as executable code by the browser.

Security headers provide an additional layer of protection against XSS attacks. The Content Security Policy (CSP) header restricts the sources from which scripts can be loaded, preventing attackers from injecting external scripts. Properly configured CSP rules can block inline scripts, mitigate script execution from untrusted domains, and enforce strict script execution policies. Other security headers, such as X-XSS-Protection and X-Frame-Options, help reduce the risk of script-based attacks by controlling browser behavior.

Modern web development frameworks provide built-in protection against XSS vulnerabilities. Many templating engines, such as Django's Jinja2 and Ruby on Rails' ERB, automatically escape user input by default. Similarly, frontend frameworks like React and Angular enforce strict data-binding rules that prevent direct manipulation of the DOM. However, developers must be cautious when using methods that override these protections, such as dangerouslySetInnerHTML in React or innerHTML in vanilla JavaScript.

Despite advances in security best practices, XSS remains a major threat due to legacy applications, poor coding practices, and evolving attack techniques. Automated scanners can help identify XSS vulnerabilities, but manual testing is often necessary to detect complex payloads and logic flaws. Security professionals perform penetration testing using tools like Burp Suite, OWASP ZAP, and custom scripts to uncover vulnerabilities before attackers can exploit them.

The consequences of XSS attacks can be severe, affecting both individual users and organizations. Attackers can steal authentication tokens, impersonate users, or perform actions on their behalf without their consent. In enterprise environments, XSS can be leveraged to escalate privileges, compromise internal systems, or exfiltrate sensitive data. Even minor XSS vulnerabilities can lead to large-scale security breaches if exploited in combination with other vulnerabilities.

Preventing XSS requires a proactive security approach, integrating secure coding practices throughout the development lifecycle. Regular security audits, code reviews, and the adoption of secure development frameworks help reduce the attack surface. As new web technologies emerge, staying informed about evolving XSS techniques and mitigation strategies remains essential for maintaining secure web applications.

Cross-Site Request Forgery (CSRF) Attacks

Cross-Site Request Forgery (CSRF) is a web security vulnerability that allows attackers to trick users into performing unintended actions on a website where they are authenticated. This type of attack exploits the trust a web application has in the user's browser, leveraging existing authentication sessions to execute malicious requests without the user's consent. CSRF attacks are particularly dangerous because they do not require the attacker to steal credentials or bypass authentication mechanisms. Instead, they rely on a user's active session with a targeted website to send unauthorized commands that the server interprets as legitimate.

A successful CSRF attack typically involves social engineering tactics to lure a victim into executing a request. This can be done through phishing emails, malicious links, or hidden scripts embedded in compromised web pages. For example, an attacker might craft an HTML form that submits a request to a banking website, transferring funds to the attacker's account. If the victim is already logged into their online banking session and unknowingly triggers this form submission, the bank's server may process the transaction without requiring further authentication, believing it to be a legitimate action by the user.

CSRF attacks rely on the way browsers handle authentication cookies and session tokens. When a user logs into a web application, their browser automatically includes authentication credentials such as cookies in every subsequent request to that website. If the application does not implement proper CSRF protections, an attacker can craft a request that the victim unknowingly submits while authenticated. Since the browser includes the victim's session cookies in the request, the server cannot distinguish between a legitimate request and a forged one. This makes CSRF particularly effective against applications that allow state-changing actions without additional verification steps.

Several factors contribute to the success of CSRF attacks. Web applications that rely solely on session cookies for authentication without additional validation mechanisms are highly vulnerable. Additionally, websites that accept requests without requiring explicit user actions, such as clicking a button or re-entering credentials, can be more susceptible. CSRF is especially dangerous when targeting sensitive actions such as changing email addresses, modifying account passwords, or performing financial transactions.

Defending against CSRF requires implementing security measures that ensure requests originate from legitimate users. One of the most effective protections is the use of CSRF tokens, which are unique, random values generated by the server and embedded in each request that modifies application state. When a request is received, the server checks for the presence and validity of the CSRF token before processing the action. Since an attacker cannot predict or access a valid

CSRF token, they are unable to forge legitimate requests on behalf of the victim. Proper token implementation involves ensuring that tokens are unique per session, included in all state-changing requests, and validated on the server side.

Another defense mechanism is enforcing the SameSite attribute on cookies. The SameSite attribute instructs browsers to restrict sending cookies along with cross-site requests, effectively preventing CSRF attacks that rely on session cookies being automatically included in malicious requests. Setting the SameSite attribute to Strict ensures that cookies are only sent when requests originate from the same domain. The Lax setting provides a balance between security and usability by allowing cookies for top-level navigations while blocking them in cross-origin requests initiated by scripts or hidden forms.

User authentication processes can also incorporate additional verification steps to mitigate CSRF risks. Multi-factor authentication (MFA) requires users to provide a second form of verification, such as a one-time passcode, before executing sensitive actions. Requiring users to re-enter their passwords or confirm actions via email or SMS further reduces the likelihood of successful CSRF attacks. Additionally, implementing CAPTCHA challenges on critical actions adds an extra layer of protection by ensuring that the request originates from a human user rather than an automated exploit.

Web applications can also leverage HTTP headers to enhance security. The Referer and Origin headers provide context about where a request originates. By validating these headers, applications can reject requests that come from untrusted sources. However, relying solely on Referer headers is not foolproof, as some browsers and network configurations may strip or modify these headers.

Developers should adopt secure coding practices to minimize CSRF risks. Frameworks and libraries that provide built-in CSRF protection should be used whenever possible. For example, many modern web frameworks automatically include CSRF tokens in form submissions and enforce token validation on the server side. Security audits, penetration testing, and code reviews should also be performed regularly to identify and mitigate CSRF vulnerabilities before they can be exploited.

Educating users about potential CSRF attack vectors is another important aspect of mitigation. Users should be cautious about clicking on untrusted links, opening email attachments from unknown sources, and executing scripts from external websites. Security awareness training can help users recognize social engineering tactics used to facilitate CSRF attacks. Organizations should also enforce strict content security policies (CSP) to prevent attackers from embedding malicious scripts within trusted domains.

CSRF remains a significant security threat due to the way web applications handle user authentication and session management. Without proper defenses, attackers can manipulate user sessions to perform unauthorized actions on behalf of victims. Implementing CSRF tokens, enforcing secure cookie policies, validating request origins, and incorporating additional authentication measures are crucial steps in mitigating CSRF risks. As web security evolves, continuous improvements in application design and user awareness will play a vital role in preventing CSRF attacks from compromising sensitive data and user accounts.

SQL Injection Attacks and Defenses

SQL injection (SQLi) is one of the most well-known and dangerous web application vulnerabilities, allowing attackers to manipulate database queries by injecting malicious SQL statements. This type of attack exploits insufficient input validation and improper handling of user-supplied data within SQL queries. When successfully executed, SQL injection can lead to unauthorized access to sensitive data, database modification, and even complete system compromise. Despite being a well-documented vulnerability, SQL injection remains a major threat due to poor coding practices and the widespread use of vulnerable legacy applications.

SQL injection occurs when an application dynamically constructs SQL queries using user input without proper validation or sanitization. A common example is a login form where an application checks user credentials by embedding input directly into an SQL query. If an attacker inputs a specially crafted string, they can manipulate the query logic and bypass authentication. For example, if a query is constructed as SELECT * FROM users WHERE username = 'input' AND password = 'input', an attacker could enter ' OR '1'='1 as the password, resulting in a query that always evaluates to true and grants unauthorized access.

The impact of SQL injection varies based on the privileges of the database user executing the query. If the application runs with administrative privileges, an attacker can modify or delete entire databases, create new user accounts, or execute system commands. Even if the attacker lacks full database control, they can still extract valuable information such as usernames, passwords, credit card numbers, or personal records. Advanced SQL injection techniques, such as blind SQL injection and time-based injection, allow attackers to exploit applications even when error messages are suppressed.

Blind SQL injection is a technique used when an application does not return database error messages but still behaves differently based on injected SQL queries. Attackers infer database behavior by analyzing response times, content changes, or redirection patterns. Time-based SQL injection is a variant where an attacker uses database functions that introduce delays, measuring response times to determine whether an injection attempt is successful. These techniques require more effort but are effective against applications that attempt to hide error messages.

To defend against SQL injection, developers must adopt secure coding practices that eliminate direct user input within SQL queries. The most effective defense is the use of parameterized queries and prepared statements, which separate SQL logic from user input. Instead of constructing queries with string concatenation, applications should use placeholders for user input, ensuring that input is always treated as data rather than executable SQL. Most modern database libraries support parameterized queries, making it straightforward to implement this defense.

Input validation is another critical layer of defense, ensuring that user input adheres to strict rules before being processed. Applications should enforce input constraints such as length limits, expected data types, and allowed characters. While input validation alone does not eliminate SQL injection risks, it significantly reduces the attack surface by preventing unexpected input formats. Additionally, applications should employ output encoding to prevent SQL meta-characters from being interpreted as part of a query.

Database security configurations play an important role in mitigating SQL injection risks. Applications should follow the principle of least privilege, ensuring that database accounts used by the application have only the necessary permissions. Running the application with a low-privilege database user limits the potential damage of a successful SQL injection attack. Security measures such as disabling unnecessary database functions, restricting direct database access, and enabling logging and monitoring help detect and prevent attacks.

Web application firewalls (WAFs) provide an additional layer of protection by filtering malicious SQL injection attempts before they reach the application. WAFs use predefined rules to identify SQL injection patterns, blocking suspicious requests in real-time. While WAFs are not a substitute for secure coding practices, they offer an extra defense mechanism against automated SQL injection attacks and zero-day vulnerabilities. Regular security assessments, including penetration testing and automated vulnerability scanning, help identify SQL injection weaknesses before attackers can exploit them.

SQL injection remains a persistent threat due to the continued use of vulnerable coding practices and outdated systems. Developers must integrate security into the entire software development lifecycle, ensuring that applications are designed to handle user input safely. By implementing secure coding standards, enforcing strict database permissions, and continuously testing for vulnerabilities, organizations can significantly reduce the risk of SQL injection attacks. Security awareness and best practices must be ingrained in development teams to ensure long-term protection against evolving threats.

Command Injection and OS Injection

Command injection and OS injection vulnerabilities arise when an application improperly handles user input, allowing attackers to execute arbitrary system commands. These attacks occur when web applications pass user-controlled input to system-level functions without adequate validation, enabling malicious actors to gain control over the underlying operating system. Unlike SQL injection, which targets databases, command injection exploits direct interactions with the operating system, potentially leading to full server compromise, data exfiltration, and further exploitation of networked systems.

Web applications often rely on system commands to perform administrative tasks such as executing scripts, retrieving system information, or managing files. If input is not properly sanitized, an attacker can manipulate these commands to execute arbitrary code. For example, a web application might use a system call to retrieve network configurations, taking user input to specify a target host. If the input is incorporated into a command string without validation, an attacker could append malicious commands to gain unauthorized access or extract sensitive data.

One of the most common exploitation techniques is appending additional commands using shell operators. Many operating systems interpret symbols such as ;, &&, and || to concatenate multiple commands in a single execution. An application that constructs a shell command like ping user_input is vulnerable if an attacker submits 127.0.0.1; rm -rf /. This input results in the server executing both the ping command and the destructive rm -rf / command, potentially wiping critical files. Similar exploits can be performed using && to execute additional commands only if the previous command succeeds, or || to execute malicious commands if the first command fails.

OS injection vulnerabilities extend beyond simple command execution. Attackers can use them to establish persistent access, escalate privileges, and move laterally within a compromised network. By injecting commands to create new user accounts, modify access permissions, or establish reverse shells, attackers can gain a foothold in the system. A reverse shell allows an attacker to establish a remote session with the server, giving them continuous access to execute commands and manipulate files at will. This level of control is particularly dangerous in environments where the web server runs with elevated privileges or has access to sensitive resources.

Defending against command injection requires strict input validation and proper use of system command execution functions. Applications should never directly incorporate user input into command strings.

Instead, developers should use parameterized functions that execute commands safely without exposing the underlying shell. Many programming languages offer system command execution functions, but they vary in their level of security. Functions such as system(), exec(), and popen() in languages like PHP and Python can be dangerous if user input is not properly handled. Using safer alternatives like subprocess.run() in Python with properly defined arguments helps prevent injection attacks by avoiding direct shell interpretation.

Another key mitigation strategy is implementing allowlists for acceptable input values. If an application must accept user input for system commands, it should limit valid options to a predefined set of safe values. For example, instead of allowing arbitrary input for a command-line utility, an application can restrict choices to specific, vetted parameters. Additionally, input sanitization techniques such as escaping special characters can reduce the risk of injection, but they should not be relied upon as the primary defense mechanism.

Server security configurations also play a crucial role in mitigating OS injection risks. Applications should run with the least privilege principle, ensuring that the web server process does not have administrative rights. Restricting execution permissions, disabling unnecessary command-line utilities, and monitoring system logs for suspicious activity help detect and prevent attacks. Intrusion detection systems (IDS) and web application firewalls (WAFs) can provide an additional layer of defense by identifying and blocking command injection attempts in real-time.

Regular security assessments, including penetration testing and automated vulnerability scanning, help identify command injection vulnerabilities before attackers can exploit them. Security researchers often use tools like Burp Suite, OWASP ZAP, and custom scripts to test for OS injection flaws by injecting various payloads and analyzing application responses. Keeping applications, frameworks, and server software updated with the latest security patches further reduces the risk of exploitation.

Command injection remains one of the most severe web security threats due to its potential impact on system integrity and confidentiality. By following secure coding practices, enforcing strict input validation, and applying the principle of least privilege, developers can significantly reduce the risk of OS injection vulnerabilities. Continuous monitoring, regular security testing, and adherence to best practices in system administration are essential for maintaining a secure web application environment.

File Upload Vulnerabilities

File upload functionality is a common feature in web applications, allowing users to submit documents, images, and other content. However, improperly secured file upload mechanisms can introduce significant security risks, including remote code execution, data leaks, and unauthorized system access. Attackers often exploit weaknesses in file validation, storage, and execution processes to compromise applications and underlying systems. Understanding these vulnerabilities and implementing proper security controls is essential to prevent malicious exploitation.

One of the primary risks associated with file uploads is the execution of arbitrary code. If an application allows users to upload executable files without proper validation, an attacker can upload a script disguised as an image or document and execute it on the server. For example, if a web application permits PHP file uploads and does not restrict execution, an attacker can upload a malicious PHP script, access it via a browser, and gain control over the server. This can lead to data breaches, privilege escalation, and system-wide compromise. Even if the uploaded file is not directly executed, attackers can exploit misconfigurations to manipulate how the server processes files, potentially triggering unintended behaviors.

Another critical vulnerability arises from insufficient file type validation. Many web applications attempt to filter malicious uploads by checking file extensions, but this approach can be bypassed. Attackers often rename executable files with permitted extensions, such as changing a .php file to .jpg to evade simple checks. Some web servers determine file types based on MIME types rather than extensions, and attackers can manipulate headers to deceive validation mechanisms. Proper file type verification should involve inspecting file contents rather than relying solely on extensions or MIME types.

Storage-related vulnerabilities also pose significant threats. If uploaded files are stored in publicly accessible directories without proper access controls, an attacker may be able to retrieve or modify them. This issue is particularly severe when dealing with sensitive documents, such as identification records or financial statements. Attackers may also use uploaded files as a means to perform directory traversal attacks, accessing restricted areas of the file system. Secure storage practices should include isolating uploaded files from publicly accessible directories and restricting direct access through controlled retrieval mechanisms.

Another common attack vector is the exploitation of metadata and embedded scripts within uploaded files. Many file formats, such as PDFs, images, and office documents, support embedded scripts or macros. Attackers can craft files containing malicious payloads that execute when opened by unsuspecting users. For example, an attacker may upload an image containing an embedded script that triggers when the image is processed by a vulnerable application. Applications should sanitize metadata and disable automatic execution of embedded content to reduce this risk.

Denial-of-service (DoS) attacks can also be carried out through file uploads. An attacker may attempt to overwhelm a server by uploading excessively large files, consuming storage space and processing power. If an application does not enforce size limits on uploaded files, it may become unresponsive or crash due to resource exhaustion. Rate limiting, file size restrictions, and proper error handling mechanisms help mitigate this risk by ensuring that malicious actors cannot abuse file upload functionality to degrade application performance.

To prevent file upload vulnerabilities, applications should enforce strict validation rules, including checking file extensions, verifying MIME types, and inspecting file contents. Uploaded files should never be stored in executable directories, and applications should avoid directly executing user-submitted files. Instead, uploaded files should be renamed with randomized names to prevent attackers from predicting and accessing them. Secure access control mechanisms should be implemented to ensure that only authorized users can retrieve uploaded files.

Modern web applications often employ sandboxing techniques to further mitigate file upload risks. Sandboxing isolates file processing from critical application components, preventing malicious files from affecting core functionality. Additionally, scanning uploaded files for malware using antivirus solutions can help detect and block known threats before they reach end users. Regular security assessments, penetration testing, and code reviews are essential to identifying and addressing file upload vulnerabilities before attackers can exploit them.

Ensuring the security of file upload functionality requires a combination of technical controls, secure coding practices, and continuous monitoring. By properly validating, storing, and processing user-submitted files, developers can reduce the risk of exploitation and protect applications from file upload-based attacks. Implementing defense-in-depth strategies, such as enforcing strict access controls, scanning for malware, and sandboxing potentially dangerous files, further strengthens the overall security posture of web applications.

Directory Traversal Attacks

Directory traversal attacks, also known as path traversal attacks, occur when an attacker exploits insufficient validation of user input to access files and directories outside the intended scope of a web application. By manipulating file paths in requests, an attacker can gain unauthorized access to sensitive system files, application configurations, or user data. This vulnerability arises when applications allow users to specify filenames or paths without properly sanitizing input, leading to unintended exposure of the underlying file system.

Web applications often provide functionalities that involve file retrieval, such as downloading reports, viewing images, or reading configuration files. If these functionalities construct file paths dynamically based on user input, attackers can attempt to manipulate the paths to escape the intended directory. A common technique involves using special character sequences like ../ (dot-dot-slash) to navigate to parent directories. For example, an application that retrieves user files from /var/www/uploads/ might accept a request specifying ../../etc/passwd, leading the server to return the system password file instead of the intended user file.

The impact of directory traversal attacks depends on the privileges of the application and the sensitivity of accessible files. In a worst-case scenario, attackers may gain access to critical system files such as configuration files, password hashes, or API keys. If write permissions are available, attackers may alter files to inject malicious code, modify access controls, or create backdoors for persistent access. Even read-only access can be dangerous if attackers obtain credentials or other sensitive information that facilitates further attacks, such as privilege escalation or lateral movement within the system.

Exploiting directory traversal vulnerabilities requires knowledge of the underlying file system structure. Attackers often use automated tools to probe for weaknesses by testing common file locations and operating system-specific paths. Windows-based servers use backslashes (\) in file paths, while Unix-based systems use forward slashes (/), allowing attackers to craft payloads specific to the target environment. Additionally, encoding techniques such as URL encoding (%2e%2e%2f) or double encoding can be used to bypass simple filtering mechanisms.

Modern web applications incorporate various countermeasures to mitigate directory traversal attacks. Proper input validation ensures that user-supplied paths do not contain special characters or sequences that allow navigation outside the designated directory. Applications should enforce strict directory restrictions, limiting file access to predefined safe locations. Using absolute paths instead of relative paths can reduce the risk of unintended file access, while implementing allowlists for permitted filenames further restricts potential exploitation.

Server-side security configurations also play a crucial role in preventing directory traversal attacks. Web servers should be configured with appropriate access controls, ensuring that application processes run with minimal privileges. Restricting file system permissions prevents unauthorized access to sensitive files, even if an attacker successfully exploits a traversal vulnerability. Logging and monitoring access attempts can help detect unusual patterns of requests, allowing administrators to identify and respond to potential attacks.

Security best practices recommend avoiding direct user input in file path construction whenever possible. Instead, applications should map user requests to predefined identifiers that correspond to actual file locations, ensuring that file retrieval mechanisms operate within controlled boundaries. Regular security audits, penetration testing, and automated vulnerability scanning help identify and remediate directory traversal vulnerabilities before they can be exploited.

Directory traversal remains a critical security concern due to the potential exposure of sensitive information and system resources. By implementing robust validation techniques, enforcing strict access controls, and regularly testing for vulnerabilities, developers can significantly reduce the risk of directory traversal attacks. Proactive security measures, combined with continuous monitoring and threat detection, help ensure that web applications remain protected against this form of attack.

Security Misconfiguration in Web Applications

Security misconfiguration is one of the most common and preventable vulnerabilities in web applications. It occurs when security settings are not properly defined, implemented, or maintained, leaving systems exposed to attacks. These misconfigurations can stem from default settings, improper permissions, unnecessary features, or incomplete security hardening. Attackers actively seek out misconfigurations to exploit weak points, gaining unauthorized access, executing arbitrary code, or exfiltrating sensitive data. The risks associated with security misconfiguration affect all components of a web application, including web servers, databases, APIs, and cloud environments.

One of the most frequent causes of security misconfiguration is the use of default credentials. Many applications, frameworks, and database management systems come with predefined usernames and passwords to facilitate setup and deployment. If these default credentials are not changed, attackers can easily gain access by using publicly known login information. Automated scanning tools frequently search for services that still use default credentials, allowing attackers to take over vulnerable systems within minutes of exposure. Changing default credentials and enforcing strong password policies is an essential step in securing any web application.

Exposed directories and files also contribute to security misconfiguration risks. Developers often leave backup files, configuration files, or database dumps in publicly accessible locations, unintentionally exposing sensitive information. Attackers can use automated tools to scan for such files and extract credentials, API keys, or system configurations. Directory listing, which allows users to view the contents of a web directory, should be disabled to prevent attackers from discovering sensitive files. Additionally, access to administrative directories should be restricted, ensuring that only authorized users can view or modify application settings.

Misconfigured permissions and overly permissive access control settings create another attack surface for adversaries. Applications that grant excessive privileges to users, services, or processes can be exploited for privilege escalation attacks. If a web application allows unauthorized users to access administrative functionalities or modify critical configurations, attackers can manipulate the system to gain full control. Implementing the principle of least privilege, where users and services are granted only the permissions they need to perform their functions, is a key measure to mitigate this risk.

Unnecessary services and features that are left enabled on production servers can also introduce security misconfiguration vulnerabilities. Web servers, application frameworks, and databases often include debugging tools, example applications, or verbose error messages by default. While these features are useful in development environments, they should be disabled in production to prevent attackers from obtaining valuable information about the system's architecture. Detailed error messages can reveal database structures, API endpoints, or software versions, helping attackers craft targeted exploits. Instead, applications should display generic error messages while logging detailed errors internally for debugging purposes.

Misconfigurations in cloud environments present an increasingly significant risk due to the widespread adoption of cloud-based services. Many organizations fail to properly configure their cloud storage, leading to publicly accessible data repositories. Misconfigured Amazon S3 buckets, Google Cloud Storage, and Azure Blob Storage have resulted in high-profile data breaches exposing millions of sensitive records. Cloud security best practices, such as restricting access to private resources, enabling encryption, and regularly auditing permissions, are necessary to prevent unauthorized access to cloud-hosted assets.

Improperly configured security headers in web applications can expose users to cross-site scripting (XSS), clickjacking, and other client-side attacks. Headers such as Content Security Policy (CSP), X-Frame-Options, and Strict-Transport-Security (HSTS) provide additional layers of protection against common web exploits. Without these headers, attackers can inject malicious scripts, steal session tokens, or trick users into interacting with fraudulent content. Ensuring that all security headers are properly configured and consistently applied across an application is an essential step in mitigating client-side risks.

Software updates and patch management also play a crucial role in preventing security misconfiguration. Many security vulnerabilities arise from outdated software components that contain known flaws. If an application relies on an outdated web server, framework, or database engine, attackers can exploit publicly disclosed vulnerabilities to compromise the system. Regularly updating software, applying security patches, and monitoring vendor advisories help reduce the attack surface created by unpatched vulnerabilities. Automated patch management solutions can streamline the process and ensure that security updates are applied promptly.

Logging and monitoring misconfigurations can hinder an organization's ability to detect and respond to security incidents. Without proper logging mechanisms, security teams may not be aware of unauthorized access attempts, system modifications, or data breaches. Logs should be configured to capture authentication events, failed login attempts, and administrative actions while being securely stored to prevent tampering. Implementing centralized log management and real-time alerting can enhance an organization's ability to detect and mitigate threats before they escalate into major security incidents.

Security misconfiguration is a persistent challenge that requires continuous attention and proactive security measures. By eliminating default credentials, restricting access to sensitive files, enforcing least privilege, disabling unnecessary features, securing cloud environments, configuring security headers, applying software updates, and maintaining robust logging, organizations can significantly reduce the risk of misconfiguration-related vulnerabilities. Security teams should conduct regular audits, penetration tests, and configuration reviews to identify and remediate potential weaknesses before attackers can exploit them.

Insecure Direct Object References (IDOR)

Insecure Direct Object References (IDOR) is a critical web application vulnerability that occurs when an application exposes internal objects, such as database records, files, or user account details, without proper access control mechanisms. This vulnerability allows attackers to manipulate object references in requests to gain unauthorized access to data or perform unauthorized actions. IDOR vulnerabilities typically arise when developers assume that users will only interact with objects assigned to them, without enforcing proper authorization checks at the backend.

A common example of IDOR involves a web application that retrieves user-specific information based on an identifier passed in the request. For instance, a URL like https://example.com/profile?user_id=1234 may be used to fetch a user's profile details. If the application does not verify whether the requesting user is authorized to view the specified profile, an attacker could modify the user_id parameter to access another user's data. This flaw can lead to exposure of sensitive information such as personal details, financial records, or private messages.

IDOR vulnerabilities are not limited to URLs. They can also occur in API requests, form submissions, and direct database queries. Web applications that use numeric or sequential identifiers are particularly vulnerable, as attackers can easily iterate through values to access unauthorized resources. Even non-numeric identifiers, such as UUIDs, can be susceptible if not properly secured, since attackers may discover valid values through brute force or information leaks.

The impact of IDOR attacks depends on the nature of the exposed data and the application's functionality. In some cases, attackers may only be able to view unauthorized information, but in more severe cases, they may be able to modify or delete records. For example, an attacker exploiting an IDOR vulnerability in a banking application could change the account_id parameter in a fund transfer request to redirect money to an unauthorized account. Similarly, IDOR flaws in content management systems can allow unauthorized users to edit or delete important files.

Mitigating IDOR vulnerabilities requires implementing robust access control mechanisms at the application level. Developers should enforce authentication and authorization checks before granting access to sensitive resources. Instead of relying solely on client-supplied identifiers, applications should verify whether the authenticated user has the necessary permissions to access the requested object. Role-based access control (RBAC) and attribute-based access control (ABAC) can further enhance security by restricting access based on predefined policies.

Using indirect references instead of direct object identifiers can help reduce the risk of IDOR attacks. Instead of exposing internal database keys in URLs or request parameters, applications can assign temporary, randomized tokens that map to specific objects. This approach prevents attackers from guessing or modifying object references to gain unauthorized access. Additionally, encrypting or hashing object identifiers can add an extra layer of security, making it more difficult for attackers to manipulate requests.

Logging and monitoring unauthorized access attempts can help detect and prevent IDOR exploitation. Applications should track access to sensitive resources and generate alerts when unusual activity is detected. Implementing rate limiting and account lockout mechanisms can also mitigate brute-force attempts to discover valid object references. Regular security assessments, including penetration testing and automated vulnerability scanning, are essential for identifying and addressing IDOR flaws before they can be exploited.

IDOR vulnerabilities remain a significant threat due to their widespread occurrence and ease of exploitation. Many high-profile data breaches have been attributed to IDOR flaws, highlighting the need for strict access control measures in web applications. By following secure coding practices, implementing proper authorization checks, and continuously testing for vulnerabilities, developers can significantly reduce the risk of IDOR attacks. Addressing these security risks not only protects user data but also strengthens the overall security posture of web applications.

Broken Access Control

Broken access control is one of the most critical security vulnerabilities affecting web applications. It occurs when an application fails to enforce proper authorization rules, allowing attackers to access, modify, or delete data they should not have permission to manipulate. This weakness often results from flawed permission models, insecure coding practices, or misconfigured access control mechanisms. Attackers who successfully exploit broken access control can escalate privileges, access unauthorized resources, or perform administrative actions without proper authorization.

One common form of broken access control is the failure to enforce authentication requirements for sensitive operations. If an application does not check whether a user is authenticated before granting access to restricted resources, attackers can directly interact with these resources by crafting requests that bypass the intended access restrictions. This issue is often seen in APIs, where endpoints are exposed without verifying the identity of the requester. If an API lacks authentication controls, an attacker can extract sensitive data, modify records, or execute unauthorized commands.

Another widespread issue is excessive privileges granted to users, services, or roles within an application. When users are assigned broad permissions by default or roles are not properly segmented, attackers who compromise an account can gain access to functionalities that should be restricted. Privilege escalation attacks often exploit this misconfiguration, allowing attackers to elevate their access from standard user accounts to administrative control. Proper role-based access control (RBAC) or attribute-based access control (ABAC) mechanisms can help limit the scope of privileges assigned to each user.

Failure to implement access control checks on server-side logic is a major cause of broken access control. Many applications rely on client-side enforcement, such as hiding admin buttons or restricting form fields in the browser, but attackers can manipulate requests using tools like Burp Suite to bypass these restrictions. If an application only relies on front-end controls without enforcing them at the backend, an attacker can forge requests to gain access to restricted operations. Server-side validation of user permissions is essential to prevent unauthorized access.

Another critical weakness arises from insecure direct object references (IDOR). This occurs when an application exposes object identifiers, such as numeric user IDs, in URLs or request parameters without verifying whether the requesting user is authorized to access the referenced object. If an attacker can modify the identifier and access another user's data, the application is vulnerable to IDOR. Proper authorization checks must be implemented to ensure that users can only interact with objects they are explicitly permitted to access.

Access control misconfigurations in cloud environments also introduce significant security risks. Many web applications rely on cloud-based storage services, where improper permission settings can lead to public exposure of sensitive data. Unrestricted access to cloud storage buckets, misconfigured access control lists (ACLs), and overly permissive API keys can allow attackers to extract confidential information or manipulate application resources. Organizations should follow the principle of least privilege, ensuring that only authorized entities have access to cloud resources.

Logging and monitoring play an essential role in detecting and preventing broken access control exploits. If an attacker attempts unauthorized actions, proper logging mechanisms can generate alerts for suspicious activity. However, many applications fail to implement sufficient logging, making it difficult to identify and respond to security incidents. Regular audits of access control policies, combined with real-time monitoring and alerting, help organizations detect and mitigate unauthorized access attempts.

Web applications should undergo regular security testing to identify and remediate broken access control vulnerabilities. Penetration testing, automated security scanning, and code reviews can uncover flaws in access control logic before attackers exploit them. Secure coding practices, such as enforcing strict role-based permissions and ensuring server-side validation of access requests, can significantly reduce the risk of unauthorized access.

The impact of broken access control can be severe, leading to data breaches, financial fraud, and system compromise. Attackers who exploit these vulnerabilities can manipulate business logic, modify sensitive records, or gain full administrative control over an application. By implementing strict access control policies, validating authorization checks at multiple layers, and continuously monitoring for security threats, organizations can protect their web applications from unauthorized access and privilege escalation attacks.

Insufficient Logging and Monitoring

Logging and monitoring are essential components of web application security, providing visibility into system activity and enabling rapid detection of malicious behavior. When logging and monitoring mechanisms are insufficient or improperly implemented, security incidents can go undetected, allowing attackers to exploit vulnerabilities for extended periods without triggering alerts. Many organizations fail to prioritize comprehensive logging, either due to performance concerns, lack of resources, or misconfigured security policies. This oversight can result in delayed incident response, increased damage from breaches, and non-compliance with regulatory requirements.

Web applications generate a vast amount of activity data, including user authentication attempts, access requests, database queries, and system errors. Proper logging ensures that these events are recorded in a structured and searchable format, allowing security teams to analyze trends and detect anomalies. Without adequate logging, organizations lack the necessary visibility to identify unauthorized access, brute force attacks, or privilege escalation attempts. Attackers often probe web applications for weaknesses, and if their activities are not logged, defenders miss critical opportunities to detect and respond before significant damage occurs.

One common issue in insufficient logging is the failure to capture security-relevant events. Many applications only log basic operational data, such as user logins and application crashes, while neglecting critical security-related actions like failed authentication attempts, privilege changes, or modifications to sensitive files. Attackers frequently exploit this lack of visibility to conduct reconnaissance and launch attacks without fear of detection. A well-configured logging system should capture both successful and failed login attempts, permission changes, API requests, and unusual system activity.

Another significant problem arises from misconfigured or overly permissive logging. Some organizations implement excessive logging without proper organization, leading to massive, unstructured log files that are difficult to analyze. When logs contain too much irrelevant information, important security events can be lost in a flood of routine activity, making it difficult for security teams to detect actual threats. Conversely, logging too little information results in blind spots where malicious activity goes unnoticed. Striking the right balance between capturing necessary details and avoiding unnecessary log noise is critical for effective security monitoring.

Failure to protect log integrity is another weakness in logging and monitoring practices. Logs are often stored in plaintext, making them vulnerable to tampering by attackers who gain access to the system. If an attacker successfully compromises a web application, they may attempt to erase or modify logs to cover their tracks, delaying detection and response efforts. Secure logging practices involve encrypting logs, using write-once storage, and implementing strict access controls to ensure that logs cannot be altered by unauthorized users.

Effective monitoring is just as important as proper logging. Logging events without an active monitoring and alerting system is ineffective, as security teams may never review the data in time to prevent or mitigate an attack. Real-time monitoring solutions use automated alerts to notify administrators when suspicious activity occurs, enabling a rapid response. For example, a spike in failed login attempts might indicate a brute force attack, while multiple access requests from an unusual location could signal a compromised account. Without proactive monitoring, these threats may go unnoticed until significant damage has already occurred.

Security information and event management (SIEM) systems enhance monitoring capabilities by aggregating logs from multiple sources, analyzing them for patterns, and generating alerts for suspicious behavior. SIEM solutions help detect complex attack patterns that may not be apparent when analyzing logs from individual systems. Organizations that lack centralized log aggregation often struggle to correlate security events across different components of their infrastructure, leading to gaps in threat detection.

Regulatory compliance is another crucial aspect of logging and monitoring. Many industry standards, such as the General Data Protection Regulation (GDPR), the Payment Card Industry Data Security Standard (PCI DSS), and the Health Insurance Portability and Accountability Act (HIPAA), mandate specific logging and monitoring practices to protect sensitive data. Failure to comply with these regulations can result in legal consequences, financial penalties, and reputational damage. Proper logging not only enhances security but also provides a verifiable record of system activity for forensic analysis in the event of a breach.

Incident response is significantly improved when robust logging and monitoring mechanisms are in place. Security teams rely on logs to investigate security incidents, determine the extent of a breach, and identify affected systems and data. Without detailed and well-organized logs, forensic investigations become challenging, and organizations may struggle to determine how an attack occurred or what data was compromised. A strong logging framework helps organizations respond to incidents quickly, contain threats, and implement remediation measures to prevent future attacks.

Implementing effective logging and monitoring practices requires a strategic approach. Organizations should define logging policies that specify what data should be captured, where logs should be stored, and how long they should be retained. Automated log analysis tools and intrusion detection systems should be used to identify threats in real time, allowing for swift action when anomalies are detected. Regular log reviews and audits help ensure that logging configurations remain effective and that potential security risks are promptly addressed.

Many high-profile security breaches could have been prevented or mitigated if proper logging and monitoring had been in place. Attackers often leave digital footprints during reconnaissance, exploitation, and data exfiltration stages, and a well-configured logging system can provide early warning signs of compromise. Organizations that prioritize comprehensive logging, secure log storage, real-time monitoring, and continuous threat analysis can significantly enhance their overall security posture. Maintaining an effective logging and monitoring strategy is not just a best practice—it is a fundamental requirement for detecting, responding to, and mitigating cyber threats in an increasingly hostile digital landscape.

Client-Side Security Testing

Client-side security testing is an essential component of web application security, focusing on vulnerabilities that affect the user's browser and front-end application logic. While much attention is given to securing server-side components, weaknesses in client-side code can expose users to various attacks, including cross-site scripting (XSS), cross-site request forgery (CSRF), session hijacking, and data leakage. Testing the security of client-side implementations helps identify potential attack vectors that adversaries can exploit to compromise user sessions, manipulate web page content, or extract sensitive information.

Modern web applications rely heavily on client-side technologies such as JavaScript frameworks, single-page applications (SPAs), and WebAssembly. These technologies enhance user experience by reducing server dependency and enabling dynamic content updates. However, they also introduce security risks, particularly when applications process user input, store data locally, or interact with third-party scripts. Security testing of client-side components must evaluate how user data is handled, whether proper input validation is enforced, and how client-side logic interacts with server-side APIs.

A key area of client-side security testing involves analyzing how the application processes and validates user input. Many attacks exploit improper input validation, leading to XSS vulnerabilities where attackers inject malicious scripts into web pages. If input fields, URL parameters, or form submissions are not properly sanitized before rendering in the browser, an attacker can execute JavaScript that steals session cookies, redirects users to phishing sites, or manipulates page content. Testing for XSS requires examining how the application encodes and outputs data, ensuring that special characters are correctly escaped and that security headers like Content Security Policy (CSP) are enforced to limit script execution.

Client-side security testing also examines how web applications handle authentication and session management. Many applications store authentication tokens in local storage or session storage, making them vulnerable to theft through XSS attacks. Unlike cookies, data stored in local storage is accessible via JavaScript, which increases the risk of exposure if an attacker gains control of the client-side environment. Security testers verify whether authentication tokens are properly secured, ensuring that sensitive credentials are not exposed in the browser's developer console or within JavaScript files loaded by the application.

Another critical aspect of testing involves evaluating how the application manages cross-origin requests. Modern web applications frequently interact with external APIs, third-party services, and cloud-based storage solutions. The implementation of Cross-Origin Resource Sharing (CORS) policies determines which domains are permitted to access resources. Weak or improperly configured CORS settings can allow attackers to retrieve sensitive data from an application when combined with other client-side vulnerabilities. Security testing should analyze the application's CORS policies to ensure that only trusted origins can make authenticated requests and that sensitive data is not exposed to unauthorized parties.

Testing for client-side security flaws also includes evaluating how the application handles sensitive data within the Document Object Model (DOM). Many web applications dynamically update content using JavaScript, modifying the DOM based on user interactions or API responses. If sensitive information such as passwords, credit card details, or authentication tokens is stored or displayed within the DOM without proper protections, attackers can extract this information through malicious scripts or browser extensions. Security testing should verify that sensitive data is not unnecessarily exposed in the DOM, console logs, or error messages.

Security testers also assess how web applications handle dependencies on third-party scripts and content delivery networks (CDNs). Many modern applications load JavaScript libraries, fonts, and stylesheets from external sources. If an attacker compromises a third-party script, they can inject malicious code that executes on all applications that depend on the compromised resource. Client-side security testing should examine whether applications use integrity attributes (subresource integrity or SRI) to verify the authenticity of external scripts and whether dependencies are regularly updated to patch security vulnerabilities.

A growing area of client-side security testing involves testing browser-based storage mechanisms such as IndexedDB, Web Storage, and service workers. While these technologies improve performance and user experience by enabling offline functionality and caching, they can introduce security risks if sensitive data is stored insecurely. Attackers who gain access to a user's session can extract stored data, manipulate cached responses, or intercept service worker communications. Security testing should ensure that sensitive data is encrypted before storage and that storage mechanisms do not expose critical user information.

Client-side security testing is a continuous process, requiring regular audits and updates as applications evolve. Modern testing methodologies include automated security scanning tools, browser-based developer tools, and manual penetration testing to identify weaknesses in JavaScript execution, input handling, and data exposure. Organizations that prioritize client-side security testing can significantly reduce the risk of user-targeted attacks, ensuring that front-end vulnerabilities do not become entry points for larger security breaches. By integrating secure coding practices, enforcing security headers, and continuously testing client-side components, developers can build web applications that provide both functionality and resilience against evolving threats.

Using Burp Suite for Web Testing

Burp Suite is one of the most widely used tools for web application security testing, providing security professionals with powerful features to identify, analyze, and exploit vulnerabilities. It serves as an interception proxy that allows testers to inspect and modify web traffic between a browser and a target application. By capturing HTTP requests and responses, Burp Suite helps security researchers assess input handling, authentication mechanisms, session management, and server-side processing. Its extensive toolset includes features for automated scanning, manual testing, and traffic manipulation, making it an essential part of penetration testing workflows.

Setting up Burp Suite begins with configuring the tool as an HTTP proxy. Web browsers or testing applications must be directed to route their traffic through Burp Suite's proxy listener, enabling the capture of all requests and responses. To analyze HTTPS traffic, Burp Suite generates a self-signed SSL certificate that needs to be installed in the browser's trusted certificate store. Once properly configured, Burp Suite acts as a middleman, allowing testers to observe and manipulate network communications in real time.

One of Burp Suite's most frequently used components is the Proxy tool, which intercepts requests and responses before they reach their intended destination. Testers can pause requests, modify parameters, inject payloads, and observe how the application processes manipulated inputs. This functionality is particularly useful for testing authentication bypass techniques, session token manipulation, and hidden API endpoints. By identifying how applications handle unexpected input, security professionals can uncover vulnerabilities such as SQL injection, cross-site scripting, and command injection.

The Repeater tool enables manual testing by allowing users to send customized HTTP requests repeatedly while observing server responses. This tool is particularly effective for testing input validation and application logic flaws. For example, if an application enforces access control through client-side mechanisms, Burp Suite's Repeater can be used to send unauthorized requests directly to the server and analyze its response. By tweaking request parameters, testers can determine whether access control mechanisms are being enforced properly.

The Intruder tool automates attack execution by sending multiple variations of a request to a target application. Testers can configure payload lists containing different inputs to test for authentication bypass, brute-force attacks, and parameter fuzzing. By analyzing response patterns, Burp Suite helps identify weak authentication schemes, hidden parameters, and input validation flaws. The Intruder's ability to execute large-scale attack simulations makes it a powerful tool for uncovering vulnerabilities that may not be immediately obvious during manual testing.

The Scanner tool performs automated security assessments by analyzing web applications for common vulnerabilities. Burp Suite's scanner can detect issues such as SQL injection, cross-site scripting, broken authentication, and security misconfigurations. While automated scanning is valuable for identifying low-hanging security flaws, manual verification is always necessary to confirm findings and assess the real impact of detected vulnerabilities. Many penetration testers use Burp Suite's scanner as an initial reconnaissance tool before conducting more detailed manual analysis.

Burp Suite also includes the Decoder and Comparer tools, which assist with encoding, decoding, and analyzing differences in web responses. The Decoder helps testers convert encoded data such as Base64, URL encoding, and hex representations, allowing for better analysis of obfuscated payloads. The Comparer tool highlights differences between HTTP responses, helping testers detect subtle changes that could indicate security flaws, such as improper access control or information leakage.

Session management testing is another critical function Burp Suite facilitates. The tool allows testers to analyze how session cookies and authentication tokens are handled by the application. By manipulating session tokens, testers can attempt session fixation attacks, hijack active sessions, or bypass authentication controls. Proper session management is essential for application security, and Burp Suite provides the necessary tools to assess weaknesses in how sessions are assigned, validated, and terminated.

Burp Suite's Extender module allows users to integrate additional security testing extensions and scripts, expanding its capabilities beyond built-in features. The Burp App Store offers a wide range of extensions for advanced vulnerability scanning, automation, and reporting. Security professionals can also develop custom extensions using Burp Suite's API, tailoring the tool to specific testing needs. This flexibility makes Burp Suite a valuable tool for both automated security assessments and deep manual penetration testing.

While Burp Suite is a powerful security testing tool, its effectiveness depends on the skill and methodology of the tester. Understanding web application architecture, HTTP protocol mechanics, and common vulnerability patterns is essential for maximizing the potential of Burp Suite. Security professionals must balance automated scanning with manual testing to identify complex vulnerabilities that automated tools may miss. Proper use of Burp Suite's suite of tools allows for comprehensive security assessments, helping organizations strengthen their web application defenses and protect sensitive data from exploitation.

Leveraging OWASP ZAP for Pentesting

OWASP Zed Attack Proxy (ZAP) is one of the most widely used tools for web application penetration testing. Developed by the Open Web Application Security Project (OWASP), it is designed to help security professionals identify vulnerabilities in web applications by intercepting, modifying, and analyzing HTTP traffic. ZAP is an open-source tool that provides both automated and manual security testing capabilities, making it an essential resource for ethical hackers, security researchers, and developers looking to improve their application security posture.

ZAP operates as a proxy server, allowing penetration testers to inspect and manipulate web traffic between a client, such as a browser, and a target application. By configuring a web browser or API client to route traffic through ZAP, security testers can analyze requests and responses, identify security weaknesses, and modify interactions to test for vulnerabilities. The interception capabilities of ZAP make it useful for discovering issues such as broken authentication, insecure session management, improper access controls, and input validation flaws.

One of the key features of OWASP ZAP is its automated scanner, which helps testers quickly assess an application for common security issues. By running an automated scan, ZAP can identify vulnerabilities such as SQL injection, cross-site scripting (XSS), security misconfigurations, and missing security headers. The scanner provides detailed reports with findings, making it easier for developers to understand and remediate security risks. While automated scanning is a useful starting point, manual testing is necessary to uncover complex vulnerabilities that may not be detected by automated tools.

The spidering functionality in ZAP allows penetration testers to map out an application's structure by following links and gathering available endpoints. This process helps testers understand the full attack surface of a web application and discover hidden pages or functionalities that may be vulnerable to exploitation. The spidering tool can be used in both passive and active modes, with passive mode analyzing existing requests without altering application behavior and active mode actively probing the application for security weaknesses.

ZAP's fuzzing capability is another valuable feature for penetration testing. Fuzzing involves sending a large number of varied inputs to an application to identify potential weaknesses in how it processes data. By injecting unexpected or malformed input into form fields, URL parameters, and API endpoints, testers can uncover vulnerabilities such as buffer overflows, input validation failures, and command injection flaws. The fuzzing tool in ZAP allows testers to customize attack payloads and analyze responses for abnormal behavior, helping identify security gaps that may be missed by conventional testing methods.

ZAP also includes a functionality called Contexts, which enables testers to define specific areas of an application for focused security testing. By grouping URLs and application components into different contexts, testers can apply different authentication settings, access controls, and scanning techniques based on the specific security requirements of each section. This feature is particularly useful for testing multi-user applications, where different roles and access levels may expose varying security risks.

ZAP's session handling features allow testers to maintain authenticated sessions while performing security testing. Many web applications rely on session cookies, tokens, or authentication headers to manage user sessions. ZAP provides session tracking and automatic handling of authentication tokens, ensuring that testers can simulate real user interactions without losing authentication state. This feature is crucial for testing session management flaws, such as session fixation, session hijacking, and improper token expiration.

The scripting engine in ZAP provides advanced users with the ability to customize and extend its functionality. Security testers can write custom scripts to automate repetitive testing tasks, manipulate HTTP requests, or create custom attack payloads. ZAP supports scripting languages such as JavaScript, Python, and Groovy, making it flexible for different testing scenarios. Custom scripts can be used to enhance automated testing, integrate with other security tools, or perform specialized security assessments tailored to specific application requirements.

ZAP's reporting capabilities make it easy for security professionals to document findings and communicate security risks to development teams. The tool generates detailed reports that outline detected vulnerabilities, affected endpoints, and recommended mitigation strategies. These reports can be customized based on the audience, providing high-level summaries for executives or technical details for developers. Effective reporting is a critical part of the penetration testing process, as it ensures that security issues are properly documented and addressed.

Integrating ZAP into continuous integration and continuous deployment (CI/CD) pipelines enhances security testing in modern development workflows. By incorporating automated security scans into the development process, teams can identify and fix vulnerabilities early in the software development lifecycle. ZAP provides command-line tools and APIs that allow seamless integration with DevSecOps workflows, enabling security testing to be performed alongside functional and performance testing. This proactive approach reduces the risk of security flaws making their way into production environments.

As web application security threats continue to evolve, the role of penetration testing tools like OWASP ZAP becomes increasingly important. Regular security assessments using ZAP help organizations identify vulnerabilities, validate security controls, and improve overall application security. By leveraging its powerful features, penetration testers can conduct thorough security evaluations and ensure that applications are resilient against modern cyber threats. Effective use of OWASP ZAP requires a combination of automated scanning, manual testing, and continuous security improvements to stay ahead of emerging risks.

Manual Testing vs. Automated Tools

Web application penetration testing relies on a combination of manual testing and automated tools to identify security vulnerabilities. Each approach has its strengths and limitations, making it essential for security professionals to understand when to apply them effectively. Manual testing provides in-depth analysis, contextual understanding, and creative exploitation techniques, while automated tools offer speed, efficiency, and scalability. Striking the right balance between these two methodologies is crucial for a comprehensive security assessment.

Manual testing is driven by human intuition and experience, allowing penetration testers to identify complex vulnerabilities that automated scanners often miss. Many security flaws, such as business logic errors, authorization bypasses, and chained exploits, require a deep understanding of the application's functionality. Automated tools can detect common vulnerabilities like SQL injection and cross-site scripting, but they often fail to interpret application-specific security risks that arise from logical inconsistencies or misconfigured access controls. Skilled testers analyze application behavior, manipulate requests, and craft payloads tailored to the specific environment, making manual testing a critical aspect of penetration testing.

One of the most significant advantages of manual testing is the ability to think like an attacker. Automated tools operate based on predefined signatures and scanning patterns, whereas a human tester can adapt, modify, and explore unique attack vectors. Security professionals leverage manual techniques to assess multi-step authentication mechanisms, API abuse scenarios, and privilege escalation attacks. By analyzing application responses, error messages, and edge cases, testers can uncover vulnerabilities that automated tools might overlook due to lack of contextual awareness.

Despite its advantages, manual testing has limitations. It is time-consuming, requires specialized expertise, and cannot scale efficiently for large applications. Security testers must invest considerable effort in analyzing source code, interacting with application components, and crafting custom attack payloads. In large-scale environments with frequent updates, manual testing alone is insufficient to maintain continuous security assessments. Automated tools help bridge this gap by providing fast and repeatable vulnerability detection across multiple assets.

Automated security tools are designed to streamline vulnerability detection by scanning applications for known security flaws. They systematically crawl websites, analyze network traffic, and generate reports detailing potential risks. These tools excel at identifying common vulnerabilities such as cross-site scripting, SQL injection, and security misconfigurations. By leveraging extensive vulnerability databases and pattern recognition, automated scanners can quickly assess large applications, reducing the time required for initial security evaluations.

Speed and efficiency are among the primary benefits of automated testing. Unlike manual testers, automated tools can perform thousands of requests within minutes, uncovering potential security issues at scale. Organizations that manage multiple web applications or have complex infrastructures rely on automated scanning solutions to maintain security visibility across their environments. Continuous integration and deployment (CI/CD) pipelines also integrate automated security testing to detect vulnerabilities before applications are deployed to production.

While automated tools offer significant advantages, they also have limitations. False positives are a common challenge, where scanners flag vulnerabilities that may not be exploitable in real-world scenarios. Security teams must manually verify findings to avoid unnecessary remediation efforts. Additionally, automated tools often struggle with complex authentication workflows, custom encryption mechanisms, and application-specific logic flaws. They may miss vulnerabilities that require nuanced exploitation techniques, such as chained attacks that involve multiple steps.

Combining manual testing with automated tools creates a balanced and effective approach to web security assessments. Automated scanners serve as the first line of defense, identifying common weaknesses and providing a broad security overview. Manual testing then refines these findings, verifying vulnerabilities, exploiting weaknesses, and uncovering risks that automation cannot detect. Security professionals integrate both methodologies to maximize coverage, ensuring that both known and unknown threats are identified.

Real-world penetration testing engagements demonstrate the need for both approaches. Automated tools provide quick insights, highlighting potential attack surfaces and misconfigurations. Manual testers then explore these findings further, analyzing edge cases and attempting exploitation techniques that scanners cannot execute. This layered approach enhances the overall security posture of web applications, combining efficiency with deep analysis to achieve comprehensive risk mitigation.

Organizations must adopt a security strategy that leverages the strengths of both manual testing and automated tools. By incorporating automated scanning into regular security assessments while maintaining dedicated manual testing efforts, security teams can address vulnerabilities proactively. Penetration testers use automated tools for reconnaissance and routine checks, reserving manual analysis for high-risk scenarios and complex application logic. This hybrid approach ensures a more thorough evaluation, reducing the likelihood of security gaps.

Web security is a constantly evolving landscape, requiring continuous adaptation and refinement of testing methodologies. Automated tools provide speed and consistency, while manual testing offers insight and creativity. By leveraging both techniques, organizations can enhance their web application security, ensuring that vulnerabilities are identified and addressed before they can be exploited.

Identifying Hidden Parameters and Endpoints

Hidden parameters and endpoints play a crucial role in web application security assessments, as they can expose sensitive functionalities that developers did not intend to be publicly accessible. Attackers and security testers alike seek to uncover these hidden components to determine whether they can be exploited to bypass authentication, retrieve confidential data, or manipulate application behavior. Identifying these elements requires a combination of manual testing, automated tools, and an understanding of how web applications structure their requests and responses.

Many web applications rely on parameters to pass data between the client and server, often through URL query strings, form fields, or API requests. While visible parameters are included in front-end interfaces and can be easily manipulated, hidden parameters may be referenced internally by the application but not displayed to users. These hidden parameters often control access to administrative features, enable debugging functionalities, or define internal configurations. Attackers attempt to identify and modify these parameters to escalate privileges, alter system settings, or expose unintended information.

Endpoints, which define accessible resources in web applications, are another key focus for security testing. Some endpoints are publicly documented, while others are kept hidden for internal use. These hidden endpoints may provide access to administrative panels, debugging utilities, or legacy features that developers have not properly secured. Attackers seek out such endpoints by analyzing application behavior, intercepting network traffic, and reviewing client-side scripts that reference non-public resources. Discovering hidden endpoints can reveal functionality that circumvents normal access controls or exposes sensitive operations.

One technique for uncovering hidden parameters is examining application responses for inconsistencies. When interacting with a web application, testers send requests with various inputs to observe how the application reacts. Unexpected behavior, such as error messages referencing undefined parameters or responses containing additional data when certain inputs are provided, can indicate the presence of hidden parameters. By crafting requests that include guessed parameter names, testers can determine whether the server recognizes and processes them, even if they are not explicitly documented.

Automated tools such as Burp Suite, OWASP ZAP, and param-mining scripts assist in the discovery of hidden parameters by systematically analyzing application traffic. These tools compare responses to identify differences when certain parameters are included or omitted. They can also test for common parameter names used across applications, such as "admin," "debug," "test," or "config," to determine if they trigger any changes in response behavior. By automating parameter discovery, security professionals can quickly identify potential attack vectors.

Hidden endpoints can be discovered through directory brute-forcing and wordlist-based enumeration. Attackers use tools like Dirb, Gobuster, and FFUF to send requests for commonly used endpoint names and analyze server responses. Many applications include hidden directories for administrative tasks, API documentation, or internal services, and misconfigurations can expose these resources to unauthorized users. If an endpoint responds with a status code indicating its existence but is not linked from the main application, it may serve as a potential entry point for further exploration.

Reviewing client-side resources such as JavaScript files, CSS stylesheets, and HTML source code often reveals references to hidden parameters and endpoints. Developers sometimes leave commented-out code, debug statements, or API calls in front-end files that provide clues about internal application structure. By examining JavaScript functions, event listeners, and network requests triggered by dynamic web applications, security testers can uncover additional paths and inputs that are not immediately visible in the user interface.

Analyzing request history and browser developer tools provides another method for identifying hidden components. Many modern browsers offer developer tools that allow users to inspect network requests, view cookies, and examine API calls made by an application. Security testers monitor these network interactions to identify endpoints that are accessed behind the scenes, particularly in single-page applications that dynamically retrieve data from backend servers.

By reconstructing and modifying these requests, hidden functionalities can be tested for security weaknesses.

Session manipulation and privilege escalation testing are also effective ways to uncover hidden parameters. Some web applications rely on session-based access controls but expose parameters that allow users to modify their level of access. By adjusting session tokens, user IDs, or permission-related parameters, testers can attempt to access restricted features. In cases where applications do not properly enforce authorization checks, attackers may discover hidden administrative controls that grant them elevated privileges.

Identifying hidden parameters and endpoints is an essential part of penetration testing, as these elements often provide access to undocumented or poorly secured functionality. By using a combination of manual analysis, automated tools, and creative testing techniques, security professionals can reveal security flaws before they are exploited by malicious actors. Continuous assessment and monitoring help ensure that web applications do not unintentionally expose sensitive resources through hidden inputs or unprotected endpoints.

Brute Forcing Login Pages

Brute force attacks on login pages are one of the most common techniques used by attackers to gain unauthorized access to web applications. This attack method involves systematically guessing usernames and passwords by submitting multiple authentication attempts until the correct credentials are found. Automated scripts and tools make this process highly efficient, allowing attackers to test thousands or even millions of combinations in a short period. Weak password policies, lack of rate limiting, and improper account lockout mechanisms can leave applications vulnerable to brute force attacks, making it essential for developers and security teams to implement proper defenses.

A typical brute force attack begins by identifying valid usernames or email addresses associated with an application. Attackers may obtain this information through data breaches, social engineering, or publicly available records. Some applications inadvertently reveal valid usernames through error messages that differentiate between incorrect usernames and incorrect passwords. Once a valid username is identified, the attacker can attempt to guess the corresponding password by iterating through a predefined list of common passwords, dictionary words, or combinations of characters.

Credential stuffing is a variation of brute force attacks that leverages previously breached username and password pairs to attempt unauthorized access. Many users reuse passwords across multiple accounts, making this technique highly effective. Attackers use automated tools to test these stolen credentials against login pages, taking advantage of users who have not updated their passwords after a breach. Since credential stuffing does not involve random password guessing, it often bypasses traditional brute force protection mechanisms that detect repeated login attempts from the same IP address.

The speed and success rate of brute force attacks depend on various factors, including password complexity, account protections, and network restrictions. Short, simple passwords are easily cracked using basic dictionary attacks, while complex passwords with a mix of uppercase and lowercase letters, numbers, and symbols require significantly more time to guess. Some attackers use more advanced methods, such as hybrid attacks, which combine dictionary words with variations and character substitutions, making them more effective against passwords that follow predictable patterns.

Many web applications fail to implement sufficient protection mechanisms against brute force attacks, leaving their authentication systems exposed. Lack of account lockout policies allows attackers to continue submitting login attempts indefinitely, significantly increasing their chances of success. Similarly, the absence of rate limiting enables attackers to flood a login page with thousands of requests in a short period without triggering any security measures. Web applications that do not monitor failed login attempts may also fail to detect ongoing brute force activity until an account has already been compromised.

Defending against brute force attacks requires implementing multiple layers of security controls. One of the most effective countermeasures is enforcing account lockout policies, where accounts are temporarily disabled after a certain number of failed login attempts. However, this approach must be balanced to prevent attackers from exploiting it for denial-of-service attacks by intentionally locking out user accounts. Implementing progressive delays, where the time between failed login attempts gradually increases, helps mitigate brute force attempts while reducing the risk of account lockouts.

Multi-factor authentication (MFA) is another critical defense mechanism that significantly reduces the effectiveness of brute force attacks. Even if an attacker successfully guesses a password, they would still need access to a secondary authentication factor, such as a one-time code sent via email, SMS, or an authentication app. MFA provides an additional layer of security that makes brute force attacks far less likely to succeed.

Captcha mechanisms can also be used to disrupt automated brute force attacks by requiring users to solve a challenge before submitting multiple login attempts. While captchas can be an effective deterrent, they must be carefully implemented to ensure they do not create usability issues for legitimate users. Some attackers use advanced bots and machine learning algorithms to bypass basic captcha challenges, making it necessary to use more sophisticated solutions that detect automated behavior.

Monitoring login attempts and detecting unusual authentication patterns are essential for identifying and mitigating brute force attacks in real time. Web applications should log failed login attempts and implement alerting systems to notify administrators of suspicious activity, such as repeated login failures from a single IP address or login attempts from unusual geographic locations. Security teams can use these logs to identify attack trends, block malicious IP addresses, and implement additional security measures as needed.

Organizations should also encourage users to adopt strong password practices by enforcing password complexity requirements and implementing password expiration policies. Educating users about the risks of password reuse and promoting the use of password managers can help reduce the likelihood of successful brute force and credential stuffing attacks. Some web applications also implement breached password detection, preventing users from selecting passwords that have previously been exposed in data breaches.

Brute force attacks remain a persistent threat to web applications, exploiting weak authentication mechanisms and poor security practices. By implementing robust security controls such as account lockouts, rate limiting, multi-factor authentication, captcha challenges, and real-time monitoring, organizations can significantly reduce the risk of unauthorized access through brute force techniques. Strengthening authentication mechanisms, promoting user awareness, and continuously monitoring login activity are essential steps in protecting web applications from credential-based attacks.

Analyzing APIs for Security Weaknesses

Application Programming Interfaces (APIs) serve as the backbone of modern web applications, facilitating communication between different systems, services, and platforms. As APIs handle sensitive data, authentication, and business logic, they become prime targets for attackers seeking to exploit security weaknesses. Understanding the vulnerabilities associated with APIs is critical for securing web applications and preventing data breaches. Security analysis of APIs involves examining authentication mechanisms, access controls, data validation, error handling, and exposure of sensitive information.

One of the most significant security risks in APIs is weak or improperly implemented authentication. Many APIs rely on API keys, tokens, or OAuth mechanisms to authenticate requests. If these credentials are exposed in public repositories, leaked through error messages, or embedded in client-side code, attackers can misuse them to access restricted data. Additionally, APIs that do not enforce strict authentication measures may allow unauthorized users to interact with endpoints, leading to unauthorized data access or system manipulation. Security testing involves verifying that authentication tokens are securely transmitted, stored, and refreshed according to best practices.

Broken access control is another common vulnerability affecting APIs. Improperly enforced authorization rules can allow attackers to access data that should be restricted to specific users or roles. This occurs when an API fails to validate whether a user has the appropriate permissions for a requested resource. Security testing involves analyzing endpoint responses with different authorization levels, attempting to access user-specific data while authenticated as a different user, and manipulating request parameters to escalate privileges. APIs should implement role-based access controls, enforce least privilege principles, and restrict data access based on user roles.

Injection attacks remain a significant concern for APIs, as user input is frequently processed and stored in backend systems. APIs that accept unvalidated input from clients may be vulnerable to SQL injection, command injection, or XML External Entity (XXE) attacks. Attackers can craft malicious payloads that manipulate database queries, execute unauthorized commands, or retrieve sensitive files. Security testing involves injecting various payloads into API request parameters, observing how the system processes the input, and identifying potential injection vulnerabilities. Proper input validation, parameterized queries, and safe parsing techniques mitigate these risks.

Exposure of sensitive data through API responses is another critical weakness that can lead to information leaks. APIs often return structured data in JSON or XML formats, and excessive data exposure can inadvertently provide attackers with insights into system internals. Security testing involves examining API responses to determine whether unnecessary data, such as internal database identifiers, debug information, or authentication tokens, is being returned. Proper response filtering, encryption of sensitive data, and enforcing the principle of minimal disclosure help reduce the risk of data leaks.

Rate limiting and throttling are essential security measures to prevent abuse of APIs. Without proper request rate controls, attackers can launch brute force attacks, enumeration attacks, or denial-of-service (DoS) attacks against an API. Security testing involves sending high volumes of requests to determine whether the API enforces rate limits and prevents excessive requests from overwhelming the system. Implementing IP-based rate limiting, user-based request quotas, and CAPTCHA challenges can help mitigate automated abuse and API misuse.

Security misconfigurations in API implementations can introduce vulnerabilities that expose systems to unauthorized access. Default configurations, misconfigured security headers, and unprotected administrative endpoints can leave APIs vulnerable. Security testing involves reviewing API documentation, testing endpoints for unnecessary exposure, and analyzing security headers such as CORS policies, content security policies, and HTTP strict transport security settings. APIs should follow secure defaults, restrict cross-origin requests, and enforce proper security headers to prevent attacks.

Error handling and logging practices also play a crucial role in API security. Poorly implemented error messages may disclose internal system details, stack traces, or database structures, providing attackers with valuable information for crafting exploits. Security testing involves intentionally triggering errors to assess how the API responds and whether excessive information is revealed. Properly configured error messages should provide minimal details while ensuring that logs capture sufficient data for monitoring and threat detection without exposing sensitive information.

API security testing must also include an assessment of third-party integrations and dependencies. Many APIs rely on external services for authentication, payment processing, or data exchange. If third-party services have security weaknesses, they can introduce risks to the application. Security testing involves analyzing API dependencies, reviewing third-party libraries for known vulnerabilities, and ensuring that external integrations follow secure communication protocols. Regular updates, vulnerability assessments, and supply chain security practices are essential for maintaining a secure API environment.

Implementing continuous API security monitoring helps detect and respond to emerging threats. Security testing should be integrated into the development lifecycle, with automated scanning tools identifying vulnerabilities in real-time. Web application firewalls (WAFs), API gateways, and security analytics platforms can provide additional layers of protection by filtering malicious traffic, detecting anomalies, and enforcing access controls. Regular security audits, penetration testing, and adherence to security best practices help ensure that APIs remain resilient against evolving attack techniques.

Cryptographic Failures in Web Applications

Cryptography plays a fundamental role in securing web applications by protecting sensitive data, ensuring confidentiality, and verifying integrity. When cryptographic mechanisms are improperly implemented, outdated, or misconfigured, they introduce vulnerabilities that attackers can exploit to intercept communication, decrypt sensitive information, or forge digital signatures. Cryptographic failures remain a leading cause of data breaches, making it critical for developers to understand common mistakes and apply best practices to safeguard web applications.

One of the most common cryptographic failures is the use of weak encryption algorithms. Older cryptographic standards such as MD5, SHA-1, and DES are no longer considered secure due to advances in computing power and cryptanalysis techniques. Attackers can crack these algorithms using brute-force attacks or precomputed hash tables, exposing sensitive information such as passwords, API keys, and personal data. Web applications that still rely on deprecated encryption methods must transition to modern cryptographic standards like AES-256 for symmetric encryption and SHA-256 or SHA-3 for hashing to maintain security.

Another significant issue arises from improper key management. Encryption is only as strong as the secrecy of the cryptographic keys, and exposing or mishandling keys renders encryption ineffective. Many breaches occur due to hardcoded keys in source code, publicly accessible configuration files, or weak key generation processes. Attackers who gain access to these keys can decrypt data, impersonate users, or manipulate encrypted sessions. Proper key management involves storing encryption keys securely using hardware security modules (HSMs) or key management systems (KMS) and rotating them periodically to minimize exposure risks.

Insecure storage of sensitive data also contributes to cryptographic failures. Web applications frequently handle confidential information such as user credentials, financial transactions, and personal records. If this data is stored in plaintext or encrypted without strong key protection, it becomes an easy target for attackers. Best practices dictate that passwords should be stored using hashing algorithms with salt and key-stretching techniques, such as bcrypt, Argon2, or PBKDF2, to increase computational resistance against brute-force attacks. Additionally, encrypting stored data with strong ciphers and implementing proper access controls helps prevent unauthorized access.

Improper use of transport layer security (TLS) weakens the confidentiality of data in transit. Many web applications still rely on outdated TLS versions, such as TLS 1.0 and TLS 1.1, which are vulnerable to attacks like BEAST, POODLE, and downgrade exploits. Even when TLS 1.2 or TLS 1.3 is used, misconfigurations such as weak cipher suites, missing certificate validation, or improper session handling can allow attackers to intercept or manipulate encrypted communications. Enforcing strict TLS configurations, disabling weak protocols, and using certificates issued by trusted certificate authorities (CAs) ensure secure data transmission between clients and servers.

Failure to properly implement cryptographic random number generation introduces predictability, making encryption and authentication mechanisms easier to break. Many security features, such as session identifiers, cryptographic salts, and API keys, rely on random values for security. If an application uses weak random number generators, attackers can predict these values and exploit vulnerabilities in session management, token generation, or key derivation. Ensuring that applications use cryptographically secure random number generators, such as those provided by modern programming libraries, strengthens security against prediction-based attacks.

Another cryptographic weakness arises from improper implementation of digital signatures and message authentication codes (MACs). Digital signatures verify the authenticity and integrity of messages, software, and transactions. When weak hash functions or incorrect key usage undermines digital signatures, attackers can forge messages or tamper with signed data. Applications that use JWTs (JSON Web Tokens) with weak signing algorithms or fail to validate signature authenticity risk token manipulation attacks. Proper implementation requires using secure signing algorithms such as RSA-PSS or ECDSA with strong key lengths and ensuring that verification steps are strictly enforced.

Developers sometimes expose cryptographic operations to side-channel attacks by failing to implement constant-time algorithms. Side-channel attacks exploit information leaks, such as execution timing differences or power consumption patterns, to extract cryptographic keys or sensitive data. Applications that perform cryptographic computations with variations in execution time, especially during password comparison or signature verification, are vulnerable to timing attacks. Implementing constant-time comparison functions prevents attackers from inferring information based on processing time discrepancies.

Another critical issue in cryptographic security is improper certificate validation in web applications and APIs. Many applications use TLS certificates to authenticate servers and encrypt traffic, but failing to validate these certificates properly exposes users to man-in-the-middle (MITM) attacks. Applications that accept self-signed certificates, ignore certificate expiration warnings, or do not verify certificate chains allow attackers to intercept and modify encrypted traffic. Implementing strict certificate validation policies and using pinned certificates can mitigate MITM risks.

Web applications that rely on custom cryptographic implementations often introduce severe security risks due to incorrect algorithm design, lack of peer review, and weak entropy sources. Many cryptographic flaws originate from developers attempting to create proprietary encryption methods instead of using well-tested industry standards. Custom cryptography often lacks the rigorous analysis required to resist modern attacks, making it an easy target for attackers. Adhering to established cryptographic libraries, such as OpenSSL, Bouncy Castle, or libsodium, ensures that encryption, hashing, and authentication mechanisms follow secure implementation standards.

Understanding and mitigating cryptographic failures is essential for securing web applications against data breaches, unauthorized access, and tampering. Adopting modern cryptographic standards, enforcing strong key management practices, securing data storage and transmission, and ensuring proper implementation of cryptographic functions help reduce risks associated with encryption weaknesses. Regular security audits, penetration testing, and compliance with cryptographic best practices ensure that web applications remain resilient against evolving threats in the cybersecurity landscape.

Vulnerable Third-Party Components

Modern web applications rely heavily on third-party components, including libraries, frameworks, and external services, to accelerate development and enhance functionality. These components provide developers with prebuilt solutions for authentication, data processing, user interface elements, and security features. However, using third-party components introduces significant security risks, especially when these dependencies contain vulnerabilities that can be exploited by attackers. Identifying and mitigating these risks is essential to maintaining the security and integrity of a web application.

One of the primary concerns with third-party components is that they may include known security vulnerabilities that can be exploited if not regularly updated. Attackers often target outdated libraries and frameworks because vulnerabilities in these components are publicly documented and easily accessible through vulnerability databases such as the National Vulnerability Database (NVD) and Common Vulnerabilities and Exposures (CVE) lists. If an application continues to use outdated components without patching, attackers can exploit known weaknesses to gain unauthorized access, execute arbitrary code, or disrupt services.

The supply chain nature of software development exacerbates the risks associated with third-party components. Many libraries and frameworks depend on other open-source or proprietary software, creating a chain of dependencies that can introduce hidden security weaknesses. A vulnerability in one component can propagate through multiple layers of dependencies, making it difficult for developers to assess the full impact on their applications. Automated dependency management tools help identify security risks by analyzing component versions and cross-referencing known vulnerabilities, but they must be actively monitored and maintained to remain effective.

Another challenge arises from the use of third-party JavaScript libraries and content delivery networks (CDNs). Many web applications load JavaScript libraries dynamically from external sources to improve performance and scalability. If an attacker compromises a third-party CDN or injects malicious code into a widely used library, all applications relying on that resource become vulnerable. These types of supply chain attacks can have widespread consequences, as seen in high-profile incidents where attackers inserted malicious payloads into popular JavaScript libraries, affecting thousands of websites. To mitigate this risk, developers should implement subresource integrity (SRI) checks, ensuring that only authorized versions of external scripts are executed in their applications.

Authentication and authorization mechanisms that rely on third-party services also introduce potential vulnerabilities. Many applications use external authentication providers, such as OAuth and OpenID Connect, to manage user logins and permissions. If these third-party services experience a security breach or are improperly configured, attackers may exploit weaknesses to bypass authentication and gain unauthorized access to protected resources. Security teams must regularly audit and validate third-party authentication implementations, ensuring that tokens are securely stored, transmitted, and validated according to best practices.

Misconfigured third-party components pose another significant risk to web applications. Many external services and libraries offer default configurations that prioritize ease of use over security. If developers do not properly configure these components, they may expose sensitive data, enable debugging features in production environments, or create insecure API endpoints. Configuration reviews and security testing help identify misconfigurations that could be exploited by attackers to extract data, execute unauthorized commands, or manipulate system behavior.

The reliance on third-party dependencies also increases the attack surface of an application, making it more difficult to maintain a comprehensive security posture. Each additional component introduces potential vulnerabilities, requiring organizations to adopt a proactive approach to dependency management. Security policies should enforce strict version control, limit the use of unnecessary components, and require regular security assessments of third-party code. Automated scanning tools, such as Software Composition

Analysis (SCA) solutions, assist in tracking and updating dependencies while alerting developers to emerging security threats.

Organizations must also consider the legal and compliance implications of using third-party components. Many open-source libraries and frameworks operate under specific licensing agreements that dictate how they can be used, modified, and distributed. Failure to comply with licensing requirements can lead to legal disputes, financial penalties, or restrictions on software distribution. Security teams should assess the licensing terms of third-party components to ensure that they align with organizational policies and regulatory requirements.

Monitoring for emerging threats in third-party components is a continuous process that requires collaboration between development, security, and IT operations teams. Regular security audits, vulnerability assessments, and penetration testing help identify weaknesses in external dependencies before attackers can exploit them. Establishing a process for promptly applying security patches and updates reduces the risk of running vulnerable software in production environments. By integrating security practices into the software development lifecycle, organizations can minimize the risks associated with third-party components while maintaining the flexibility and efficiency they provide.

Web applications must balance the benefits of third-party components with the security challenges they introduce. While external libraries and frameworks accelerate development and provide essential functionality, they also create new entry points for attackers if not properly managed. Organizations that prioritize dependency security, enforce strict access controls, and continuously monitor third-party integrations can reduce the risk of exploitation and strengthen their overall security posture.

Session Fixation and Cookie Security

Session fixation is a web security vulnerability that allows an attacker to take control of a user's session by forcing them to use a known session identifier. This type of attack exploits weaknesses in session management mechanisms where a web application fails to properly regenerate session identifiers upon user authentication. If an attacker can trick a user into using a predefined session ID, they can later take control of that session once the user logs in, gaining unauthorized access to the account. Effective session management practices are necessary to prevent this type of attack and ensure that user sessions remain secure.

A common scenario for session fixation involves an attacker obtaining a valid session ID before the victim logs in. The attacker then tricks the victim into using that session ID by embedding it in a malicious link or injecting it into the victim's browser through other means, such as phishing emails or cross-site scripting (XSS). If the web application does not issue a new session ID upon authentication, the attacker can later reuse the same session identifier to gain access to the authenticated session. Since the server still considers the session valid, the attacker can impersonate the victim without needing their login credentials.

Preventing session fixation requires applications to generate a new session ID whenever a user logs in. This ensures that any previously issued session identifiers become invalid, preventing an attacker from hijacking an active session. Secure applications enforce session regeneration by invalidating old session tokens and assigning fresh ones immediately after authentication. Proper session lifecycle management also includes ensuring that session identifiers cannot be reused after logout or prolonged inactivity.

Cookie security plays a vital role in protecting session management mechanisms, as session identifiers are often stored in cookies. Weak cookie configurations can expose session tokens to unauthorized access, increasing the risk of session fixation, session hijacking, and other attacks. Secure attributes such as HttpOnly, Secure, SameSite, and proper expiration settings help protect cookies from theft and unauthorized access by malicious scripts or network-based attacks.

The HttpOnly attribute prevents JavaScript from accessing cookies, reducing the risk of session theft through XSS attacks. When this attribute is set, client-side scripts cannot read or manipulate the session token, making it harder for attackers to extract it from a compromised browser session. This is particularly important for preventing malicious scripts injected through vulnerabilities like stored or reflected XSS from stealing authentication tokens and sending them to an attacker's server.

The Secure attribute ensures that cookies are only transmitted over encrypted HTTPS connections. Without this setting, session cookies may be exposed in plaintext over unencrypted HTTP requests, allowing attackers to intercept and steal them using man-in-the-middle (MITM) attacks. Applications that enforce HTTPS-only communication should always mark session cookies as Secure to prevent exposure over insecure connections.

The SameSite attribute restricts how cookies are sent with cross-origin requests, mitigating the risk of cross-site request forgery (CSRF) attacks. When set to Strict, cookies are only sent in first-party requests, preventing them from being included in requests initiated by external websites. The Lax setting provides a balance between security and usability by allowing cookies in top-level navigations while blocking them in cross-site subrequests. Properly configured SameSite attributes help prevent attackers from tricking authenticated users into performing unintended actions on a vulnerable web application.

Session expiration policies also play a crucial role in session security. Sessions that remain active indefinitely increase the risk of unauthorized access, especially if users do not log out properly. Implementing session timeout mechanisms based on inactivity ensures that idle sessions automatically expire after a predefined period. Additionally, enforcing absolute session expiration limits prevents long-lived sessions from being exploited even if they remain active.

Improper session storage can also lead to security vulnerabilities. Storing session identifiers in local storage or session storage rather than cookies exposes them to JavaScript-based attacks. Unlike cookies with the HttpOnly attribute, storage mechanisms such as local storage are accessible by client-side scripts, making them more susceptible to theft through XSS. Web applications should always store session tokens in secure, server-issued cookies rather than relying on local storage methods.

Session fixation and cookie security are closely related to other web security practices, including authentication mechanisms, encryption standards, and access controls. Proper session handling ensures that attackers cannot predict, reuse, or manipulate session identifiers to gain unauthorized access. By implementing secure cookie attributes, enforcing session expiration policies, and regenerating session identifiers upon authentication, web applications can effectively mitigate the risks associated with session fixation attacks and unauthorized session access. Regular security audits, penetration testing, and adherence to best practices help maintain a secure session management framework that protects user data and authentication processes.

Business Logic Flaws

Business logic flaws are vulnerabilities that arise from the improper implementation of an application's intended functionality. Unlike traditional security weaknesses that stem from technical misconfigurations or outdated software, these flaws exploit the logical flow of a system to manipulate how it processes requests, enforces rules, or executes business operations. Attackers leverage these weaknesses to gain unauthorized access, bypass restrictions, or perform unintended actions within the application. Identifying and mitigating business logic flaws requires a deep understanding of the application's workflows, rules, and expected behaviors.

A common example of a business logic flaw occurs in e-commerce applications where attackers manipulate payment or discount mechanisms. Some systems allow users to apply multiple discount codes to a single transaction, reducing the total cost to an unintended amount. In other cases, attackers exploit race conditions by submitting multiple requests simultaneously, tricking the application into processing duplicate discounts or generating additional store credits. These attacks do not rely on traditional vulnerabilities like injection flaws or misconfigured permissions but instead exploit gaps in the logic that governs transactions.

Authentication and authorization mechanisms are also frequent targets of business logic attacks. Some applications fail to enforce proper user role validation, allowing attackers to escalate privileges by modifying request parameters. For example, an attacker may change an account ID in a request to gain access to another user's information, circumventing intended access controls. If an application does not correctly verify a user's authorization level before executing critical actions, malicious users can manipulate the system to perform actions reserved for administrators or privileged accounts.

Business workflows that involve sequential approval processes are vulnerable to logic-based exploitation if they do not properly track and enforce dependencies. For example, in financial applications, attackers may attempt to withdraw funds before a deposit is fully verified, leading to unauthorized transactions. Similarly, in multi-step approval processes, attackers may find ways to bypass intermediary steps by modifying request flows or altering session states. These types of attacks require a detailed understanding of how data is processed within the application and how rules are enforced at each stage.

Session handling flaws can also result in business logic vulnerabilities when applications fail to enforce proper session expiration policies. Some systems allow users to remain authenticated indefinitely, even after changing account permissions or performing security-sensitive actions. Attackers may take advantage of these gaps to maintain access to privileged features after their authorization has been revoked. Proper session management ensures that authentication states are updated dynamically based on role changes, logouts, or security policies.

Rate limiting and abuse prevention mechanisms play a crucial role in mitigating business logic attacks. Applications that rely on resource-intensive operations, such as account registration, order processing, or search functionalities, can be manipulated by attackers who automate requests at scale. Without appropriate throttling controls, attackers can overload systems, create excessive accounts, or manipulate transaction rates to disrupt normal operations. Implementing request limits, CAPTCHA mechanisms, and behavioral analysis helps prevent automated abuse and logic-based exploitation.

Business logic flaws are particularly dangerous because they are application-specific and often evade traditional security scanning tools. Automated vulnerability scanners focus on detecting common misconfigurations, injection flaws, and insecure dependencies, but they are not designed to analyze the logical flow of an application's business rules. Identifying these flaws requires manual security testing, threat modeling, and an in-depth review of how the application enforces its intended functionality.

Attackers often discover business logic vulnerabilities by analyzing how an application processes user input and executes workflows. Security testers use penetration testing techniques to simulate real-world attacks, attempting to manipulate data flows, bypass validation mechanisms, and exploit inconsistencies in logic enforcement. By testing for unexpected behaviors and edge cases, security teams can uncover flaws that may not be immediately obvious in normal usage scenarios.

Defending against business logic flaws requires a combination of secure coding practices, robust validation mechanisms, and continuous monitoring of application behavior. Developers should implement strict validation rules to ensure that user input aligns with expected business logic requirements. Additionally, enforcing strong access controls, tracking session states, and implementing request integrity checks help mitigate the risks associated with logic-based attacks. Regular security reviews, penetration testing, and collaboration between development and security teams are essential for identifying and addressing business logic flaws before attackers can exploit them.

Applications that handle financial transactions, account management, and sensitive business operations must take additional precautions to protect against logic-based attacks. Implementing fraud detection systems, anomaly detection algorithms, and real-time monitoring solutions helps identify suspicious behavior before it causes significant damage. By integrating security into the application development lifecycle, organizations can proactively address business logic flaws and maintain the integrity of their systems.

Exploring Web Application Firewalls

Web Application Firewalls (WAFs) are an essential security measure designed to protect web applications from a wide range of cyber threats. These firewalls operate by monitoring and filtering HTTP traffic between a client and a web server, identifying and blocking malicious requests before they can reach the application. Unlike traditional firewalls, which primarily focus on network-layer security, WAFs analyze application-layer traffic to detect vulnerabilities such as SQL injection, cross-site scripting (XSS), and other attacks targeting web applications. Proper implementation and configuration of a WAF significantly enhance an organization's ability to defend against common threats while ensuring application availability and integrity.

One of the primary functions of a WAF is inspecting incoming traffic for patterns that indicate malicious activity. WAFs use predefined rule sets and anomaly detection techniques to identify attacks, allowing legitimate traffic while blocking or mitigating harmful requests. These rules can be based on signature matching, behavioral analysis, or machine learning models that detect suspicious patterns in web requests. For example, a WAF can recognize and block SQL injection attempts by identifying suspicious query structures that do not align with typical user input. Similarly, XSS prevention mechanisms within a WAF detect and neutralize scripts attempting to execute unauthorized code in a user's browser.

WAFs operate in different modes depending on an organization's security needs. In monitoring mode, the WAF logs and analyzes traffic but does not actively block requests, allowing security teams to observe attack attempts without disrupting legitimate traffic. In blocking mode, the WAF actively prevents malicious requests from reaching the application, reducing the risk of exploitation. Some WAFs also offer hybrid deployment models, allowing organizations to test rule sets in monitoring mode before enforcing stricter security policies. This flexibility helps prevent false positives, ensuring that legitimate users are not mistakenly blocked while still protecting against real threats.

Cloud-based WAF solutions provide an additional layer of security by protecting applications at the network edge, mitigating distributed denial-of-service (DDoS) attacks and large-scale automated threats. These WAFs are integrated with content delivery networks (CDNs), reducing the load on the application server while filtering malicious requests before they reach the backend infrastructure. Organizations that deploy cloud-based WAFs benefit from continuous updates, as security providers regularly update rule sets to defend against new attack vectors. However, cloud-based WAFs require careful configuration to balance security and performance, ensuring that legitimate traffic is not unnecessarily delayed or blocked.

Self-hosted WAFs offer greater customization and control over security policies, making them ideal for organizations with specific compliance requirements or highly sensitive data. These WAFs can be deployed as hardware appliances, software-based solutions, or integrated directly within web servers. While self-hosted WAFs provide in-depth configurability, they require ongoing maintenance, tuning, and threat intelligence updates to remain effective against evolving attack techniques. Security teams must regularly review logs, adjust rule sets, and analyze attack trends to optimize protection without introducing operational inefficiencies.

Attackers continuously develop techniques to bypass WAF protections, making it necessary for security teams to refine their configurations and adapt to emerging threats. Some attackers evade WAF detection by encoding payloads, using alternative character sets, or modifying HTTP request headers to bypass signature-based detection mechanisms. To counter these tactics, modern WAFs incorporate behavior-based anomaly detection, artificial intelligence-driven threat analysis, and automated learning models that adapt to new attack patterns over time. Regular security assessments and penetration testing help identify weaknesses in WAF configurations, ensuring that security policies remain effective.

WAFs also play a crucial role in regulatory compliance and data protection. Many security standards, such as the Payment Card Industry Data Security Standard (PCI DSS) and the General Data Protection Regulation (GDPR), require organizations to implement strong web security controls. Deploying a WAF helps organizations meet these compliance requirements by providing real-time monitoring, logging, and mitigation of web-based threats. Security logs generated by WAFs serve as valuable forensic data, aiding in incident response and threat investigation processes.

Integration with other security tools enhances the effectiveness of WAFs in defending against sophisticated attacks. Many organizations combine WAFs with intrusion detection systems (IDS), security information and event management (SIEM) solutions, and endpoint protection platforms to establish a multi-layered security approach. By correlating data from different sources, security teams gain deeper insights into attack trends, enabling proactive threat mitigation strategies. Automation capabilities within modern WAF solutions also allow security teams to respond to threats in real time, dynamically adjusting firewall rules based on detected attack behavior.

While WAFs provide a strong defense against web application attacks, they should not be relied upon as a standalone security measure. A comprehensive web security strategy includes secure coding practices, regular vulnerability assessments, proper access controls, and robust authentication mechanisms. Organizations that implement a WAF alongside other security best practices create a more resilient security posture, reducing the risk of application breaches and data exposure. Continuous monitoring, rule tuning, and security updates ensure that WAFs remain effective in an ever-evolving threat landscape.

Bypassing WAFs and Filters

Web Application Firewalls (WAFs) and filtering mechanisms are designed to protect web applications from various types of attacks by analyzing and blocking malicious traffic. They act as a defense layer against threats such as SQL injection, cross-site scripting (XSS), and command injection. However, skilled attackers and penetration testers continuously develop techniques to bypass these security measures. Understanding the weaknesses of WAFs and how attackers evade them is critical for improving web application security and ensuring that defensive mechanisms are properly configured.

One of the most common techniques used to bypass WAFs involves encoding payloads in ways that alter their appearance without changing their functionality. Many WAFs rely on pattern matching to detect malicious input, and encoding methods such as URL encoding, Base64 encoding, or hexadecimal representation can sometimes evade detection. Attackers manipulate payloads by encoding special characters or using alternate representations of keywords to avoid triggering security rules. For example, instead of directly injecting an SQL statement using the UNION keyword, an attacker might encode it as %55%4E%49%4F%4E, which some poorly configured WAFs may fail to recognize as malicious.

Another technique involves using case variation and obfuscation to evade pattern-based detection. Some WAFs apply strict filtering to certain keywords but fail to detect variations in capitalization or spacing. Attackers can manipulate queries by using mixed-case payloads, inserting comments between characters, or adding whitespace in unexpected ways. For example, a SQL injection attempt using UNION SELECT could be rewritten as UnIoN/**/SeLeCt, effectively bypassing a WAF that only blocks exact matches of the keyword UNION SELECT.

Attackers also leverage different encoding schemes and alternate representations of characters to trick WAFs into allowing malicious input. Unicode encoding and double encoding are frequently used to bypass filters that only block standard ASCII representations. By encoding special characters using UTF-8 or other formats, attackers can construct payloads that appear harmless to the WAF while still being interpreted correctly by the target application. This technique is particularly effective against poorly configured or outdated WAFs that do not normalize input before analysis.

In some cases, attackers take advantage of discrepancies between how a WAF processes input and how the backend application interprets it. Many WAFs attempt to detect attacks by applying rule-based filtering to HTTP requests, but if the backend server processes input differently, attackers can craft payloads that bypass the firewall while still executing successfully. This is commonly seen in SQL injection attacks, where different database engines interpret certain characters differently. An attacker may use alternate string concatenation techniques or database-specific syntax to evade detection by a generic WAF rule.

Bypassing WAFs also involves exploiting how security rules handle request fragmentation and reassembly. Some WAFs analyze input based on predefined tokenization patterns, which can be disrupted by splitting a payload across multiple requests or using chunked encoding. By sending payloads in fragmented pieces, attackers can evade detection mechanisms that rely on full-string matching. This technique is particularly effective against WAFs that do not properly reassemble fragmented requests before performing security checks.

Some attackers use request smuggling techniques to bypass WAF protection by taking advantage of inconsistencies in how different web servers and proxies process HTTP headers. Request smuggling manipulates HTTP header formats in a way that causes the backend server to interpret a request differently than the WAF does. By carefully crafting headers, attackers can slip malicious payloads through a firewall that only analyzes the initial request structure without correctly parsing all variations.

Another method of bypassing WAFs is leveraging trusted sources or whitelisted IP addresses. Many organizations configure their WAFs to allow traffic from known or internal sources without applying strict security rules. Attackers who gain access to a trusted network or hijack an internal IP address can bypass the WAF entirely by appearing as a legitimate user. This highlights the importance of monitoring internal traffic and ensuring that security controls apply to all request sources, not just external ones.

Security testing tools such as Burp Suite, SQLmap, and WAF-bypass scripts provide penetration testers with automated techniques for identifying and evading WAF defenses. These tools use a combination of encoding, obfuscation, and request manipulation to probe for weak points in filtering rules. When conducting penetration testing, security teams analyze how a WAF responds to different attack attempts, identifying misconfigurations that could allow real-world exploits. Proper tuning of WAF rules based on actual attack patterns strengthens protection against bypass techniques.

Despite advancements in WAF technology, no filtering mechanism is completely immune to bypass attempts. Attackers continuously adapt their strategies, finding new ways to evade detection. The most effective way to defend against bypass techniques is to implement a multi-layered security approach that combines WAF protection with secure coding practices, input validation, and behavior-based anomaly detection. Security teams must regularly test and update WAF rules to address emerging threats, ensuring that web applications remain protected against evolving attack methods.

Understanding CSRF Token Mechanisms

Cross-Site Request Forgery (CSRF) is a web security vulnerability that exploits the trust between a user and a web application. Attackers use this technique to trick users into performing unintended actions on a website where they are authenticated. A successful CSRF attack can lead to unauthorized fund transfers, data modifications, or even account takeovers. To mitigate these attacks, modern web applications implement CSRF token mechanisms, which act as an additional layer of security to ensure that requests originate from legitimate users and not from malicious sources.

CSRF attacks rely on the automatic transmission of authentication credentials, such as cookies, session tokens, or stored authentication headers. When a user is logged into a web application, the browser automatically includes these credentials in every request made to that application. If an attacker can trick the user into unknowingly submitting a request, the server may process it as a legitimate action, as it sees the request as coming from an authenticated user. This exploitation is particularly dangerous in applications that allow state-changing actions, such as updating account settings, modifying permissions, or performing financial transactions.

CSRF token mechanisms serve as a primary defense against these attacks by introducing an additional piece of information that the attacker cannot easily obtain. A CSRF token is a unique, unpredictable value generated by the server and associated with a user session. When a user submits a form or performs a sensitive action, the CSRF token must be included in the request. The server validates this token before processing the request, ensuring that it originated from the legitimate user interface and not from an attacker-controlled source. If the token is missing or incorrect, the request is rejected.

The effectiveness of CSRF tokens depends on their proper implementation. The token must be unique per user session or per request to prevent reuse by attackers. If an application generates predictable or static CSRF tokens, attackers can anticipate them and craft malicious requests that include valid tokens. Proper token generation uses cryptographically secure random values that cannot be easily guessed. Additionally, CSRF tokens should be tied to the user's session to prevent attackers from injecting valid tokens into victim requests.

Secure storage and transmission of CSRF tokens are also critical to their effectiveness. Tokens are typically embedded in HTML forms as hidden input fields or included as custom headers in AJAX requests. When using cookies for session management, CSRF tokens should not be stored in cookies themselves, as an attacker could retrieve them through cross-site scripting (XSS) attacks. Instead, tokens should be delivered as part of server-rendered pages or fetched securely via an authenticated API endpoint. Proper token validation on the server side ensures that only requests with valid tokens are processed.

Web applications that use JavaScript-heavy front-end frameworks, such as React or Angular, must implement CSRF token handling for API interactions. Since these applications rely on API calls rather than traditional form submissions, CSRF tokens should be included in the request headers. Many modern frameworks provide built-in support for CSRF protection by automatically retrieving and attaching tokens to AJAX requests. Proper integration of CSRF tokens within API-based workflows ensures that client-side applications remain protected against forged requests.

An alternative mitigation technique involves using the SameSite cookie attribute, which restricts when cookies are sent with cross-site requests. When set to Strict, cookies are only sent when the request originates from the same domain, effectively preventing CSRF attacks. The Lax setting allows cookies to be sent in top-level navigations but not in background requests, providing a balance between security and usability. While SameSite cookies reduce CSRF risks, they do not eliminate the need for CSRF tokens in applications that require broader compatibility or support cross-origin interactions.

CSRF protection mechanisms should be combined with other security controls to create a robust defense strategy. Applications should enforce strong authentication measures, including multi-factor authentication (MFA), to prevent unauthorized access even if a CSRF attack is attempted. Logging and monitoring CSRF validation failures can help detect attack attempts and inform security teams of potential threats. Security best practices, such as implementing Content Security

Policy (CSP) headers and sanitizing user input, further strengthen an application's resilience against CSRF and related attack vectors.

Proper implementation and validation of CSRF tokens are essential for web application security. Developers must ensure that tokens are generated securely, stored safely, and validated correctly in every state-changing request. By integrating CSRF tokens with secure authentication mechanisms, enforcing SameSite cookie policies, and adopting modern security frameworks, web applications can effectively prevent CSRF attacks and maintain the integrity of user actions. Regular security audits and penetration testing help identify weaknesses in CSRF protection mechanisms, ensuring that applications remain secure against evolving threats.

Security Issues in Single Page Applications (SPAs)

Single Page Applications (SPAs) have become a popular architecture for modern web applications due to their seamless user experience and efficient front-end interactions. Unlike traditional multi-page applications, SPAs dynamically update the content of a webpage without requiring full reloads. This design improves performance and user engagement but also introduces unique security risks. Because SPAs rely heavily on JavaScript, APIs, and client-side logic, attackers have a broader surface area to exploit vulnerabilities such as cross-site scripting (XSS), API abuse, improper authentication mechanisms, and exposure of sensitive data.

One of the most significant security concerns in SPAs is cross-site scripting (XSS). Since SPAs rely on client-side rendering and heavy JavaScript execution, improper input handling can lead to XSS vulnerabilities where attackers inject malicious scripts into the application. These scripts can steal session tokens, manipulate the Document Object Model (DOM), or execute unauthorized actions on behalf of users. Unlike traditional server-rendered applications that can enforce strict content security measures, SPAs often process and display dynamic content directly in the browser. If input is not properly sanitized and escaped, malicious payloads can be injected and executed, compromising user accounts and application integrity.

Implementing strong Content Security Policy (CSP) headers and ensuring proper input validation across all client-side operations help mitigate these risks.

Authentication and session management present another security challenge for SPAs. Many SPAs rely on JSON Web Tokens (JWTs) or OAuth-based authentication instead of traditional session cookies. While these mechanisms provide flexibility in handling authentication across multiple services, improper storage of authentication tokens can lead to serious security vulnerabilities. Some applications store tokens in local storage or session storage, which are accessible through JavaScript. If an attacker successfully exploits an XSS vulnerability, they can extract authentication tokens and hijack user sessions. A more secure approach is to store authentication tokens in HTTP-only cookies, which cannot be accessed by client-side scripts, reducing the risk of theft through XSS attacks.

APIs serve as the backbone of SPAs, handling data retrieval, authentication, and business logic. Weak API security is a common issue in SPA-based architectures, as APIs are often exposed to the public internet. If API endpoints do not enforce proper authorization checks, attackers can manipulate API requests to access or modify unauthorized data. Rate limiting, input validation, and proper authentication mechanisms such as OAuth 2.0 help protect against API abuse and ensure that sensitive data remains secure. Additionally, API responses should avoid exposing excessive information about internal systems, as attackers can use this data to craft more targeted attacks.

Client-side business logic is another security concern in SPAs. Since much of the application logic is executed on the client side, attackers can analyze and manipulate JavaScript code to bypass security controls. If sensitive business logic, such as pricing calculations, access control rules, or encryption algorithms, is exposed in client-side scripts, attackers can modify the code to gain an unfair advantage. Obfuscating JavaScript code and performing critical security checks on the server side instead of the client helps prevent such attacks.

Cross-Origin Resource Sharing (CORS) misconfigurations can introduce vulnerabilities in SPAs that interact with APIs hosted on different domains. If CORS policies are too permissive, attackers can craft malicious websites that trick users into making unauthorized requests to a vulnerable API. Improperly configured CORS headers allow attackers to read sensitive responses and steal user data. Secure CORS configurations should restrict allowed origins, enforce authentication measures, and prevent unauthorized websites from accessing protected resources.

State management in SPAs can also lead to security risks if not properly implemented. Many SPAs rely on client-side state management libraries such as Redux or Vuex to store user data and application state. If sensitive information, such as authentication tokens or user roles, is stored in the application state without proper encryption, attackers can extract and manipulate this data. Secure state management practices involve minimizing the exposure of sensitive data on the client side and using encrypted, server-validated mechanisms for handling user sessions and privileges.

The dynamic nature of SPAs introduces another challenge related to security headers and browser protections. Traditional web applications benefit from built-in security headers that enforce protections such as X-Frame-Options, Content Security Policy (CSP), and Referrer-Policy. However, SPAs often load content dynamically through AJAX requests and may not enforce these headers consistently. Missing or misconfigured security headers can make an application more vulnerable to attacks such as clickjacking, information leakage, and data exfiltration. Regularly auditing security headers and enforcing them across all application responses strengthens the security posture of SPAs.

SPAs also face risks related to dependency vulnerabilities. Many modern front-end applications rely on third-party JavaScript libraries and frameworks to manage functionality. If these libraries contain security vulnerabilities, attackers can exploit them to compromise the entire application. Keeping dependencies up to date, monitoring for security advisories, and using tools such as dependency scanning and software composition analysis help reduce the risk of attacks that leverage known vulnerabilities in third-party components.

Securing SPAs requires a comprehensive approach that combines secure coding practices, robust API security, proper authentication mechanisms, and regular security assessments. Developers must ensure that input validation, secure storage of tokens, and API authorization checks are implemented correctly to prevent exploitation. Adopting a defense-in-depth strategy that includes CSP enforcement, secure session management, and strict CORS policies strengthens SPA security and reduces the likelihood of successful attacks. Regular security testing, including penetration testing and code reviews, helps identify and remediate vulnerabilities before they can be exploited in real-world scenarios.

Mobile Web Application Security

Mobile web applications have become an integral part of everyday life, providing users with access to services from banking and e-commerce to social media and enterprise platforms. However, as mobile applications handle vast amounts of sensitive user data, they have become prime targets for cyberattacks. Securing mobile web applications requires addressing unique risks associated with mobile environments, including insecure data storage, weak authentication mechanisms, insufficient transport security, and vulnerabilities introduced by third-party integrations.

One of the primary security concerns for mobile web applications is the way they handle authentication and session management. Many mobile apps rely on persistent sessions to enhance user experience, often keeping users logged in for extended periods. If session tokens are not properly managed, attackers can hijack active sessions through token theft or replay attacks. Secure applications implement short-lived session tokens combined with multi-factor authentication to minimize the impact of stolen credentials. Proper token storage is also essential, as storing sensitive tokens in local storage or within unprotected databases makes them accessible to attackers if a device is compromised.

Transport layer security plays a crucial role in protecting mobile web applications from man-in-the-middle attacks. Users frequently connect to mobile applications over public Wi-Fi networks, where attackers can intercept unencrypted traffic. Without strong encryption, login credentials, API keys, and personal data can be exposed to malicious actors. Ensuring that all communications between the mobile application and backend servers are encrypted using the latest versions of TLS prevents data interception. Additionally, certificate pinning helps prevent attackers from using forged certificates to impersonate legitimate servers.

Insecure data storage is another significant issue in mobile web applications, as sensitive information may be stored on the device itself. Mobile devices are more susceptible to loss, theft, or malware infection compared to traditional desktops. Applications that store passwords, session tokens, or financial data in plaintext make it easier for attackers to extract and misuse that information. Secure storage solutions, such as encrypted keychains for iOS and the Android Keystore system, provide a more secure way to handle sensitive data on mobile devices. Encrypting local databases and restricting file system access further minimizes the risk of unauthorized data extraction.

Third-party integrations introduce additional security challenges in mobile web applications. Many apps rely on external SDKs and APIs for payment processing, analytics, social media login, and other functionalities. If these third-party components contain security flaws, they can become a weak link in the application's security posture. Attackers often target vulnerable SDKs to gain access to sensitive data or manipulate app behavior. Regular security assessments of third-party components, along with strict permissions and sandboxing techniques, help mitigate the risks introduced by external dependencies.

Mobile applications also face security risks from client-side vulnerabilities, such as cross-site scripting (XSS) and insecure web views. Web views are commonly used to render web content within mobile applications, but if they are not properly secured, they can be exploited to execute malicious JavaScript. Allowing unrestricted JavaScript execution within a web view exposes applications to data theft and phishing attacks. Developers should enforce strict content security policies, disable unnecessary scripting capabilities, and validate user input to prevent these types of client-side attacks.

The mobile threat landscape is constantly evolving, requiring continuous security monitoring and threat detection. Many organizations deploy mobile threat detection (MTD) solutions to identify malicious activities, such as unauthorized data access, abnormal network behavior, and exploit attempts. Logging and monitoring mechanisms help detect potential security breaches early, allowing developers to respond swiftly to mitigate threats. Regular penetration testing and security audits ensure that mobile web applications remain resilient against emerging attack techniques.

Security best practices for mobile web applications emphasize the importance of user awareness and secure development principles. Educating users about security risks, such as phishing attacks, malicious app installations, and safe browsing habits, helps reduce the likelihood of successful exploitation. Developers must also follow secure coding practices, implement strict access controls, and ensure that sensitive operations are performed in a protected environment. By continuously updating security policies and adapting to new threats, organizations can safeguard mobile web applications from cyber threats while maintaining usability and performance.

Exploiting Weaknesses in CORS Policies

Cross-Origin Resource Sharing (CORS) is a security mechanism implemented by web browsers to control how web applications hosted on one domain can interact with resources from another domain. This policy is essential for preventing malicious websites from making unauthorized requests to protected APIs or sensitive endpoints. However, misconfigurations in CORS policies can introduce severe security risks, allowing attackers to bypass same-origin restrictions and access confidential data. Understanding how CORS weaknesses can be exploited is critical for securing web applications against unauthorized cross-origin requests.

A common CORS misconfiguration involves allowing any origin to access sensitive resources by using a wildcard * in the Access-Control-Allow-Origin header. While this setting is sometimes used for public APIs that do not handle sensitive data, applying it to endpoints that require authentication can lead to severe security breaches. When a web server permits any origin, an attacker can craft a malicious website that tricks users into making authenticated requests to the vulnerable application. If the response includes sensitive information, the attacker's domain can read the data, effectively bypassing the browser's same-origin policy.

Some applications attempt to implement dynamic CORS policies by reflecting the Origin header sent by the client. This is often done to allow cross-origin access for trusted domains while blocking unapproved requests. However, an insecure implementation that blindly reflects any Origin header without validation can allow attackers to specify their own malicious domain as the origin. This grants them unauthorized access to API responses, enabling data theft and session hijacking. Proper validation must ensure that only pre-approved domains are allowed, preventing attackers from abusing this feature.

CORS misconfigurations are particularly dangerous when combined with other vulnerabilities such as cross-site scripting (XSS). If an application is vulnerable to XSS, an attacker can inject malicious scripts into a trusted web page, allowing them to send cross-origin requests that exploit a weak CORS policy. This attack scenario enables attackers to extract session tokens, API keys, or user data without requiring direct interaction from the victim. Ensuring that CORS policies are correctly configured is not sufficient if other client-side vulnerabilities remain unpatched.

Preflight requests, which use the OPTIONS HTTP method, serve as a security measure to verify whether a cross-origin request is permitted before it is executed. Some web servers incorrectly respond with overly permissive headers to these requests, allowing attackers to bypass security restrictions by sending specially crafted preflight requests. For example, a vulnerable server might allow credentials to be sent with cross-origin requests by including Access-Control-Allow-Credentials: true without properly verifying the requesting domain. If an attacker can exploit this misconfiguration, they can execute unauthorized actions on behalf of an authenticated user.

Credentialed requests introduce another attack surface in CORS security. When Access-Control-Allow-Credentials is set to true, browsers include authentication tokens, such as cookies and HTTP headers, in cross-origin requests. This setting should never be used in combination with a wildcard * origin, as it allows any website to make authenticated requests to the server. Attackers who control a malicious domain can exploit this flaw to access sensitive data or perform actions on behalf of the victim. Restricting credentialed requests to specific trusted origins ensures that authentication tokens are not exposed to unauthorized domains.

APIs that process sensitive operations, such as financial transactions or user account modifications, should enforce strict CORS policies to prevent abuse. A poorly configured CORS policy can allow an attacker to initiate state-changing requests from an untrusted domain, leading to account takeovers or unauthorized modifications. Ensuring that CORS rules align with an application's security model is essential to prevent these types of attacks. Proper logging and monitoring of CORS-related requests help detect potential abuse before it escalates into a full security breach.

Security best practices for CORS involve explicitly defining allowed origins, restricting HTTP methods and headers, and ensuring that authentication credentials are not exposed to unauthorized domains. Applications should maintain an allowlist of trusted domains rather than dynamically reflecting origins, reducing the risk of CORS abuse. Developers must regularly review their CORS configurations to prevent inadvertent exposure of sensitive resources. Implementing security headers such as Content Security Policy (CSP) and Referrer-Policy further strengthens defenses against cross-origin attacks, providing additional layers of protection.

Exploiting weaknesses in CORS policies can lead to severe consequences, including unauthorized data access, session hijacking, and privilege escalation. Attackers continuously look for misconfigurations that allow them to bypass same-origin restrictions, making it critical for developers to enforce strict security controls. A well-configured CORS policy, combined with secure authentication mechanisms and thorough application security testing, helps prevent cross-origin exploitation while maintaining the necessary flexibility for legitimate cross-domain communication.

Advanced Cross-Site Scripting Techniques

Cross-Site Scripting (XSS) is one of the most persistent and dangerous vulnerabilities affecting web applications. It allows attackers to inject malicious scripts into web pages viewed by other users, enabling data theft, session hijacking, and even full account compromise. While basic XSS attacks rely on simple payloads executed within a vulnerable input field, more advanced techniques bypass modern security measures and exploit complex browser behaviors. Understanding these sophisticated methods is essential for both attackers and defenders to anticipate threats and implement effective countermeasures.

One of the more advanced XSS techniques involves exploiting poorly configured Content Security Policy (CSP) headers. CSP is designed to mitigate XSS by restricting the execution of inline scripts and defining trusted sources for JavaScript execution. However, misconfigured CSP rules can still allow attackers to execute malicious scripts. For example, if a policy includes unsafe-inline or allows wildcard (*) sources, an attacker may be able to inject JavaScript through a manipulated script tag or a third-party domain. Additionally, CSP bypass techniques such as using JSONP endpoints, WebAssembly, or SVG-based scripts can enable attackers to execute malicious code despite security policies intended to prevent it.

Another method of executing XSS is through DOM-based attacks, which exploit JavaScript's dynamic behavior in the browser rather than traditional server-side injection points. In a DOM-based XSS attack, the malicious payload is processed entirely in the client's browser, often through JavaScript functions that handle user input without proper sanitization. This can occur when applications use document.write(), innerHTML, or eval() to dynamically update page content based on URL parameters, cookies, or local storage. Attackers craft payloads that manipulate the DOM in unexpected ways, executing scripts that may evade traditional filtering mechanisms.

Mutation-based XSS is another advanced technique that leverages how browsers interpret and modify injected HTML content before rendering it. Some modern browsers automatically sanitize or rewrite certain HTML elements, which can lead to unintended script execution. Attackers take advantage of this behavior by injecting seemingly harmless attributes or tags that mutate into executable scripts when processed by the browser. This technique is particularly effective in web applications that rely on JavaScript frameworks with complex rendering logic, where security controls may not anticipate how the framework handles specific payloads.

Polyglot XSS attacks use carefully crafted payloads that function across multiple encoding contexts, making them more difficult to detect and filter. Traditional XSS defenses rely on context-aware encoding, such as escaping characters within HTML attributes or JavaScript strings. However, polyglot payloads are designed to execute regardless of the encoding method applied. For instance, a payload might be structured in a way that executes within both an HTML attribute and a JavaScript function, ensuring that even partial sanitization does not neutralize the attack. This approach increases the chances of bypassing security mechanisms that only filter for specific encoding patterns.

Cross-site scripting can also be used in conjunction with other vulnerabilities to enhance the impact of an attack. For example, combining XSS with Cross-Site Request Forgery (CSRF) allows an attacker to execute actions on behalf of an authenticated user without their knowledge. Similarly, leveraging XSS in an environment where session cookies lack the HttpOnly flag enables attackers to steal authentication tokens, leading to session hijacking. In some cases, attackers use XSS to bypass same-origin policy (SOP) restrictions, exfiltrating sensitive data from another origin by manipulating how the browser processes requests.

Another sophisticated approach involves bypassing client-side security frameworks that attempt to filter malicious input. Some web applications implement JavaScript-based sanitization libraries to prevent XSS, but these libraries can often be bypassed using encoding tricks, event handlers, or unexpected HTML structures. Attackers test different variations of payloads to find weaknesses in the filtering logic, exploiting inconsistencies between how different browsers interpret security policies. By understanding how these security measures operate, attackers refine their payloads to maximize effectiveness while minimizing detectability.

Advanced XSS techniques also include targeting browser extensions, injecting scripts that manipulate browser behavior beyond a single web page. Some poorly designed extensions allow untrusted scripts to interact with privileged APIs, enabling attackers to gain deeper access to user sessions, stored credentials, or sensitive data. Similarly, attackers may use XSS to inject malicious content into web applications that interact with local resources, such as file upload tools or clipboard access functionalities. By exploiting these secondary attack surfaces, XSS can become a launching point for broader system compromise.

The rise of WebSockets and other real-time communication technologies has introduced new avenues for XSS attacks. Unlike traditional HTTP requests, WebSockets allow for continuous bidirectional communication between clients and servers, often bypassing conventional input validation mechanisms. Attackers can use XSS to inject payloads into WebSocket messages, persisting malicious scripts that execute every time data is retrieved from the server. This persistence makes it difficult to detect and remove injected scripts, particularly in applications with dynamic content rendering.

Defending against advanced XSS techniques requires a combination of secure coding practices, content security enforcement, and continuous security testing. Developers must implement strict CSP headers without insecure configurations, sanitize user input at multiple layers, and avoid insecure JavaScript functions that process dynamic content. Regular security audits and penetration testing help identify XSS vulnerabilities before they can be exploited, ensuring that web applications remain resilient against evolving attack techniques.

Social Engineering and Phishing with Web Apps

Social engineering and phishing attacks have become some of the most effective ways for attackers to exploit human vulnerabilities in web applications. These attacks manipulate users into divulging sensitive information, such as login credentials, financial data, or personal details, by impersonating trusted entities. Unlike traditional hacking techniques that rely on exploiting software vulnerabilities, social engineering targets human psychology, making it a formidable challenge for organizations to defend against. Web applications serve as both the medium and the target of these attacks, as attackers use deceptive techniques to trick users into compromising their security.

Phishing attacks often begin with carefully crafted messages that appear legitimate but are designed to manipulate victims into taking specific actions. Attackers create fake login pages that closely resemble those of well-known web services, tricking users into entering their credentials. These credentials are then captured and used for unauthorized access. Email phishing remains the most common vector, where attackers send fraudulent messages claiming to be from banks, government agencies, or corporate IT departments, urging recipients to reset passwords, verify accounts, or confirm transactions. Web applications are frequently abused in these attacks by hosting phishing pages that mimic real services, exploiting user trust to collect valuable information.

Spear phishing, a more targeted form of phishing, takes this attack a step further by tailoring messages specifically to individuals or organizations. Attackers research their targets, often using publicly available information from social media, corporate websites, or previous data breaches, to craft highly convincing messages. These messages may appear to come from colleagues, business partners, or executives, increasing the likelihood of victims falling for the deception. By using web applications as part of the attack chain, such as embedding malicious links in seemingly legitimate business communications, attackers can bypass traditional email security filters and increase their chances of success.

Another common social engineering tactic involves exploiting web-based communication channels, such as live chat systems, support portals, or social media platforms. Attackers pose as customers, employees, or technical support representatives to manipulate users into revealing information or performing unauthorized actions. In some cases, attackers convince customer service representatives to reset passwords or disable multi-factor authentication on legitimate accounts, gaining access without needing to crack passwords. These attacks highlight the importance of strict verification procedures in web applications that handle sensitive user requests.

Credential harvesting through web apps extends beyond phishing emails. Attackers set up fake online services that promise free access to premium content, job offers, or security scans. These services require users to sign up or log in using their existing credentials from other platforms, unknowingly exposing their information. Many users reuse passwords across multiple sites, making it easier for attackers to exploit stolen credentials across different web applications. By leveraging convincing branding and user interfaces, attackers make these fraudulent services appear genuine, increasing the likelihood of user engagement.

Man-in-the-middle attacks can also be used to execute social engineering-based phishing. Attackers intercept user requests to legitimate web applications, modifying responses to redirect victims to malicious login pages. Public Wi-Fi networks are a common attack surface, where unsuspecting users access their online accounts through compromised connections. Without proper encryption and validation mechanisms, web applications may inadvertently assist attackers by failing to verify the authenticity of user requests and responses.

Many phishing attacks exploit weaknesses in web application security controls, such as missing HTTPS enforcement, lack of email authentication mechanisms, and poorly implemented multi-factor authentication. Attackers register domains that closely resemble real websites, using homograph techniques where characters are replaced with visually similar Unicode symbols. These look-alike domains deceive users into believing they are interacting with the legitimate service. Web applications must implement domain validation mechanisms and educate users on how to recognize fraudulent URLs.

Some phishing campaigns leverage social media platforms and online advertisements to distribute malicious links. Attackers create sponsored ads that lead users to fraudulent login pages, exploiting trust in well-known ad networks. In other cases, attackers use compromised accounts on social media to distribute phishing links, relying on the credibility of the original account owner. Since web applications often integrate with social media for authentication and sharing, attackers use these integrations to spread malicious content further, amplifying their reach.

Defending against phishing and social engineering attacks requires a multi-layered approach that combines user education, technical security measures, and continuous monitoring. Web applications should enforce strong authentication mechanisms, including multi-factor authentication, to reduce the impact of stolen credentials. Email authentication protocols, such as SPF, DKIM, and DMARC, help prevent attackers from spoofing legitimate domains in phishing emails. Organizations should also conduct phishing awareness training for employees and users, teaching them how to recognize and report suspicious activity.

Security teams must continuously test and refine their defenses against social engineering attacks. Red teaming exercises, where security professionals simulate phishing campaigns within an organization, help identify weaknesses in user awareness and technical controls. Implementing real-time monitoring and anomaly detection in web applications allows for the identification of suspicious login attempts, rapid credential stuffing attacks, and unusual user behaviors indicative of compromised accounts.

The evolving nature of social engineering and phishing tactics means that attackers constantly adapt their methods to bypass security measures. By combining deception, technical exploitation, and psychological manipulation, they continue to find new ways to compromise users and web applications. Organizations must remain vigilant, continuously improving their security posture to stay ahead of emerging threats in the ever-changing landscape of web-based social engineering attacks.

Advanced SQL Injection Techniques

SQL injection remains one of the most dangerous and widely exploited vulnerabilities in web applications. Attackers leverage weaknesses in input validation and database queries to manipulate an application's backend database, extracting sensitive data, modifying records, or even executing system commands. While basic SQL injection attacks involve inserting malicious queries into input fields, advanced techniques allow attackers to bypass security measures, extract hidden information, and escalate privileges. Understanding these advanced attack vectors is essential for penetration testers and security professionals to strengthen database security.

One of the more sophisticated SQL injection techniques involves blind SQL injection, which occurs when an application does not return error messages but still executes queries in the background. Attackers use time-based or boolean-based inference techniques to extract information from the database. In a boolean-based blind attack, an attacker submits queries that return different responses based on true or false conditions, allowing them to deduce the content of the database one character at a time. Time-based attacks rely on SQL functions such as SLEEP() in MySQL or WAITFOR DELAY in SQL Server to measure response times and infer data from the system. These attacks are slow but effective against applications that suppress error messages.

Out-of-band SQL injection is another advanced technique that exploits database interactions with external systems. Some databases allow outbound network connections, and attackers can use this feature to exfiltrate data by making DNS or HTTP requests to attacker-controlled servers. By injecting queries that force the database to perform lookups on an external domain, attackers can retrieve sensitive information even if the application does not display query results. This method is particularly effective against heavily secured applications that block traditional SQL injection attempts but still allow outbound traffic.

Error-based SQL injection remains a powerful technique for applications that expose database error messages. Some developers fail to disable verbose error reporting, which can reveal database structure, table names, and even query contents. Attackers craft malicious input to intentionally trigger errors and extract valuable information from the resulting messages. In some cases, functions such as CAST(), CONVERT(), or division-by-zero operations force the database to return detailed error messages, providing attackers with insights into query execution.

Second-order SQL injection attacks occur when user input is stored in the database and later executed in a separate context. Unlike traditional SQL injection, where malicious input is executed immediately, second-order attacks involve injecting payloads into stored fields that remain dormant until a subsequent database query triggers them. This technique is particularly effective when applications store user data without proper sanitization and later use it in dynamically constructed queries. Attackers may inject SQL commands into registration forms, comments, or user profile fields, waiting for the application to unknowingly execute them at a later time.

Advanced SQL injection techniques also target specific database functionalities, such as leveraging stored procedures, exploiting database-linked servers, or abusing database management functions. Some databases support the execution of operating system commands through SQL queries, allowing attackers to gain shell access or execute arbitrary scripts. For example, MySQL's SELECT LOAD_FILE() function can be abused to read sensitive system files, while SQL Server's xp_cmdshell can execute Windows commands. Attackers use these capabilities to pivot from database exploitation to full system compromise.

Defensive measures against advanced SQL injection attacks involve a combination of secure coding practices, input validation, and database security configurations. Using parameterized queries and prepared statements eliminates the possibility of injecting malicious SQL code, as user input is treated strictly as data rather than executable commands. Restricting database permissions ensures that even if an injection attack occurs, the attacker cannot escalate privileges or access unauthorized tables. Regular security audits, penetration testing, and database monitoring help detect and mitigate SQL injection vulnerabilities before they can be exploited by attackers.

Exploiting XML External Entities (XXE)

XML External Entity (XXE) attacks exploit weaknesses in how web applications process XML input, allowing attackers to manipulate XML parsers to read files, make network requests, and even execute code. This vulnerability arises when an application improperly handles XML input containing external entity references, which can be leveraged to access sensitive data, perform server-side request forgery (SSRF), or trigger denial-of-service conditions. Many applications rely on XML for data exchange, configuration files, and API interactions, making XXE a critical security risk when improperly mitigated.

An XXE attack typically begins when an attacker submits a malicious XML payload to a vulnerable parser. If the parser is configured to process external entities, it will attempt to resolve the provided reference, potentially exposing system files or making unauthorized requests. This behavior is particularly dangerous in applications that accept XML uploads, SOAP-based web services, and legacy systems that have not been updated with secure parsing configurations. Exploiting XXE can allow an attacker to extract sensitive information such as configuration files, API keys, and credentials stored on the server.

One of the most well-known impacts of XXE is local file inclusion (LFI), where an attacker can use external entities to read arbitrary files on the system. By referencing system paths such as /etc/passwd on Linux or C:\Windows\win.ini on Windows, attackers can retrieve sensitive information. If the application outputs the parsed XML response, the contents of these files may be disclosed directly to the attacker. The severity of this vulnerability depends on the permissions of the application, as some processes run with elevated privileges, allowing access to restricted files.

XXE can also be leveraged for server-side request forgery (SSRF), where the attacker tricks the XML parser into making requests to internal or external systems. By specifying a malicious external entity that points to an internal IP address or a remote web service, attackers can exfiltrate data, interact with internal applications, or scan private network resources. This technique is particularly dangerous in cloud environments and containerized architectures, where attackers can use XXE to access metadata services that contain security tokens and other sensitive information.

Out-of-band (OOB) XXE attacks take the exploitation further by using external references to exfiltrate data to a remote server. Instead of retrieving and displaying the contents of a file directly within the application, the attack payload instructs the XML parser to send the extracted data to an attacker-controlled server. This method is useful in cases where the application does not return the XML response but still processes the malicious entity in the background. Attackers use this technique to bypass security filters that monitor direct file inclusion attempts, making it a stealthier approach to data exfiltration.

XXE attacks can also lead to denial-of-service (DoS) conditions by exploiting recursive entity expansion, commonly referred to as a billion laughs attack. This attack involves defining multiple nested entities that expand exponentially when parsed, consuming system resources and causing the application to crash. By submitting an XML payload with excessive entity references, attackers can overload memory and CPU usage, disrupting services and rendering the application unresponsive. This form of attack is particularly damaging in environments where XML parsing occurs on high-traffic endpoints or within shared infrastructure.

Mitigating XXE vulnerabilities requires disabling the processing of external entities within XML parsers. Secure configurations should explicitly prevent the resolution of external references by using security features provided by modern XML libraries. Many programming languages and frameworks offer options to disable DTD parsing, restrict external entity resolution, and enforce strict validation rules. Developers must ensure that XML parsing libraries are updated to the latest versions, as older implementations often contain security flaws that allow XXE exploitation.

Alternative data formats, such as JSON, can also help mitigate XXE risks by eliminating the need for XML processing. Many modern applications have transitioned to JSON-based APIs, reducing their exposure to XXE vulnerabilities. However, for applications that must support XML, implementing secure parsing practices and conducting regular security assessments are essential. Penetration testing, static code analysis, and automated security scanning help identify and remediate XXE vulnerabilities before attackers can exploit them.

Web application firewalls (WAFs) and intrusion detection systems (IDS) can provide additional protection against XXE attacks by monitoring for malicious XML payloads. Security teams should establish logging and alerting mechanisms to detect suspicious XML input, enabling rapid response to potential threats. Implementing proper access controls, network segmentation, and least privilege principles further limits the impact of successful XXE exploitation, reducing the risk of sensitive data exposure and internal network compromise.

Organizations must remain vigilant in securing XML-based applications, as XXE attacks continue to pose a significant threat across various industries. By enforcing secure parsing practices, eliminating unnecessary XML features, and adopting alternative data formats where possible, businesses can protect their systems from the devastating consequences of XXE exploitation.

Web Sockets Security Testing

WebSockets have become an essential part of modern web applications, enabling real-time communication between clients and servers. Unlike traditional HTTP-based communication, WebSockets provide full-duplex, persistent connections that allow for continuous data exchange. This technology is widely used in chat applications, stock trading platforms, collaborative tools, and online gaming. While WebSockets improve performance and interactivity, they also introduce security risks that must be carefully assessed. Testing WebSocket security involves analyzing how connections are established, whether data transmission is properly secured, and how authentication and authorization mechanisms are enforced.

One of the primary concerns in WebSocket security is the initial handshake process, which uses HTTP before upgrading the connection to WebSocket. This handshake is vulnerable to manipulation if not properly secured, especially if it allows untrusted origins to initiate connections. Attackers can exploit weak handshake implementations to establish unauthorized WebSocket sessions, gaining access to sensitive data or sending malicious commands. Proper security testing involves intercepting and modifying handshake requests to determine whether unauthorized access is possible.

Once a WebSocket connection is established, data transmission between the client and server is continuous. Unlike traditional HTTP requests, WebSocket messages do not follow the same stateless principles, making them susceptible to issues such as session fixation and token leakage. If authentication tokens or session identifiers are transmitted within WebSocket messages without encryption, attackers can intercept them and hijack user sessions. Testing for these vulnerabilities requires inspecting WebSocket traffic to identify whether sensitive data is being exposed in plaintext.

Cross-site WebSocket hijacking is another attack vector that must be evaluated during security testing. If a web application allows WebSocket connections to be initiated from any origin without proper validation, an attacker can create a malicious website that forces a victim's browser to open an unauthorized WebSocket session. This type of attack is similar to cross-site request forgery (CSRF) but specifically targets WebSocket connections. Security testers analyze how WebSocket requests handle origin validation and whether the application enforces strict cross-origin policies to prevent unauthorized interactions.

Data integrity and injection attacks are also major concerns when testing WebSocket security. Since WebSockets transmit data in real time, an attacker who gains access to the communication channel can inject malicious payloads into messages. This can result in SQL injection, cross-site scripting (XSS), or command injection attacks depending on how the application processes WebSocket messages. Security testing involves crafting and sending specially formatted messages to determine whether input validation is enforced on both client and server sides.

Man-in-the-middle attacks pose a significant risk if WebSocket connections are not encrypted using Secure WebSockets (WSS). When WebSockets operate over unencrypted channels, attackers can intercept and modify messages in transit. This can lead to data theft, session hijacking, or unauthorized command execution. Security testers verify whether WebSocket implementations enforce the use of WSS and analyze whether any downgrade attacks are possible. Ensuring that strict transport security policies are applied helps mitigate these risks.

Authorization flaws in WebSocket implementations can allow attackers to perform unauthorized actions by manipulating WebSocket messages. If role-based access controls are not strictly enforced, an attacker with limited access may be able to escalate privileges by sending unauthorized WebSocket commands. Security testing should include attempts to modify user roles, execute privileged actions, and bypass authorization checks. Applications should implement robust access control mechanisms to validate each WebSocket request based on the user's authenticated session.

Testing WebSocket security also involves analyzing how errors and exceptions are handled. Improper error handling can expose sensitive system details, such as stack traces, database queries, or internal server configurations. Attackers can use this information to craft more targeted exploits. Security testers should deliberately trigger errors by sending malformed WebSocket messages to observe how the application responds. Proper error handling ensures that minimal information is disclosed while maintaining system stability.

WebSockets remain a powerful tool for real-time communication, but their security must be thoroughly assessed to prevent exploitation. By evaluating handshake processes, testing for data leakage, enforcing strict origin policies, validating input, securing transport channels, and implementing robust authorization controls, organizations can mitigate the risks associated with WebSocket vulnerabilities. Regular security testing, combined with best practices in secure development, ensures that WebSocket-based applications remain resilient against evolving threats.

Reporting and Documentation Best Practices

Effective reporting and documentation are essential components of any penetration testing or security assessment process. While identifying vulnerabilities is critical, the ability to clearly communicate findings, remediation steps, and overall security posture to stakeholders determines the true value of a penetration test. Well-structured documentation ensures that security teams, developers, and executives can understand the risks, prioritize fixes, and implement long-term security improvements. Without proper reporting, even the most thorough penetration test loses its effectiveness, as the impact and urgency of vulnerabilities may not be conveyed properly.

A comprehensive penetration test report includes several key sections that guide the reader from a high-level overview to technical details. The executive summary provides a non-technical assessment of the test results, highlighting critical vulnerabilities and their potential impact on business operations. This section is designed for executives and decision-makers who need a quick understanding of security risks without diving into technical specifics. A clear and concise executive summary helps organizations allocate resources effectively by prioritizing the most significant threats.

The methodology section explains the approach taken during the penetration test, detailing the scope, testing techniques, and tools used. By documenting the methodology, security teams ensure transparency and reproducibility, allowing future assessments to follow similar testing procedures. This section also serves as a reference for compliance audits, demonstrating that industry-standard methodologies were used during the engagement. Organizations that adhere to regulatory frameworks such as PCI DSS, HIPAA, or ISO 27001 benefit from detailed methodology documentation to meet compliance requirements.

Detailed findings make up the core of a penetration test report. Each finding should include a description of the vulnerability, how it was discovered, the potential impact if exploited, and recommendations for remediation. Clear categorization of findings, such as critical, high, medium, or low severity, helps organizations prioritize fixes based on risk level. Well-documented findings provide supporting evidence, such as proof-of-concept exploits, screenshots, or request/response captures, making it easier for developers and security teams to verify and address issues. The language used in this section should balance technical accuracy with readability, ensuring that different audiences can interpret the information effectively.

Remediation guidance is a crucial part of security documentation. A penetration test report should not only identify vulnerabilities but also provide actionable recommendations for mitigation. These recommendations should be specific, practical, and tailored to the organization's technology stack. Where possible, multiple remediation options should be provided, considering factors such as feasibility, cost, and potential impact on business operations. In addition to immediate fixes, reports should include long-term security best practices to prevent similar vulnerabilities from reappearing in the future.

Supporting appendices enhance the usability of a penetration test report by providing additional technical details that may not be necessary for all readers. These may include full lists of tested assets, raw test results, command outputs, or detailed attack chains used to exploit vulnerabilities. Including this level of detail ensures that security teams can reference exact test conditions, aiding in verification and internal security reviews. Well-structured appendices keep the main report concise while still providing comprehensive information for those who need it.

The importance of clear and structured documentation extends beyond penetration testing reports. Security teams should maintain internal records of previous assessments, remediation efforts, and recurring vulnerabilities to track improvements over time. Historical documentation helps organizations measure security progress, identify patterns in security weaknesses, and refine their testing methodologies. Establishing a standardized format for security reports and internal documentation improves consistency, making it easier for teams to compare findings across different assessments.

Automation can play a role in improving reporting efficiency without sacrificing quality. Tools that generate structured reports based on scan results, vulnerability databases, and testing frameworks help standardize findings and reduce manual effort. However, automated reports should always be reviewed and supplemented by human testers to ensure accuracy and context. The combination of automation and human expertise creates a more effective documentation process, where reports remain both detailed and actionable.

A well-documented security assessment also facilitates knowledge sharing across teams. Developers benefit from clear remediation steps, security teams gain insights into potential attack vectors, and executives receive the information needed to make risk-based decisions. Organizations that integrate security reporting into their software development lifecycle (SDLC) create a proactive security culture, addressing vulnerabilities before they become critical issues.

Effective reporting and documentation enhance the overall impact of penetration testing by ensuring that security findings translate into measurable improvements. By structuring reports with clear summaries, detailed findings, actionable remediation steps, and supporting documentation, organizations can maximize the value of security assessments. Standardized reporting practices, combined with automation and continuous knowledge sharing, strengthen long-term security resilience while enabling teams to address vulnerabilities in a structured and efficient manner.

Leveraging Bug Bounty Platforms

Bug bounty platforms have transformed the landscape of cybersecurity by allowing organizations to crowdsource security testing through ethical hackers. These platforms enable companies to identify vulnerabilities in their applications before malicious actors can exploit them. By offering financial incentives and public recognition, organizations attract skilled security researchers who actively probe their systems for weaknesses. Unlike traditional penetration testing, which is limited by time and resources, bug bounty programs provide continuous security assessments from a diverse pool of testers with varying expertise.

One of the key advantages of bug bounty platforms is the extensive range of testing they provide. Organizations benefit from the collective knowledge and creativity of security researchers across the globe, exposing their applications to real-world attack scenarios that may not be covered by internal security teams. Researchers bring different perspectives, using unique testing methodologies to uncover vulnerabilities that automated scanners and structured assessments might miss. This diversity enhances security coverage, ensuring that even subtle logic flaws or obscure misconfigurations are identified.

Bug bounty programs operate under structured guidelines, defining the scope of testing, eligible targets, and acceptable attack techniques. Companies must carefully outline these parameters to ensure that ethical hackers focus on authorized areas while avoiding disruption to critical services. Clearly defined rules help prevent unintended security incidents and guide researchers on what types of vulnerabilities are most valuable. Organizations also determine reward structures based on the severity and impact of reported vulnerabilities, encouraging researchers to prioritize findings that pose the greatest risk.

Coordinating an effective bug bounty program requires an efficient vulnerability triage and response process. Security teams must evaluate submissions quickly, verifying the legitimacy and impact of reported issues. Delayed responses or unclear communication with researchers can discourage participation and reduce the program's effectiveness. Many bug bounty platforms provide built-in workflows that facilitate communication between security teams and researchers, ensuring that vulnerabilities are addressed promptly and that researchers receive feedback on their findings.

For organizations new to bug bounty platforms, starting with a private program can provide a controlled testing environment. Private programs invite a select group of experienced researchers to test an application before opening it to a broader audience. This approach allows companies to refine their internal response processes, validate their security posture, and gradually scale their program. Once confidence in the security maturity of the application is established, transitioning to a public bug bounty program can attract a larger pool of researchers and yield more comprehensive results.

One challenge organizations face when running bug bounty programs is managing duplicate or low-quality reports. Popular platforms often have many researchers testing the same targets, leading to multiple submissions of the same vulnerability. To mitigate this issue, companies implement clear policies on how duplicates are handled and use automated tools to track previously reported issues. Encouraging researchers to conduct thorough testing and submit well-documented reports improves efficiency, allowing security teams to focus on critical vulnerabilities rather than minor misconfigurations or false positives.

The financial aspect of bug bounty programs is another consideration. Companies must allocate a budget that reflects the value of the vulnerabilities being reported. High-impact security flaws demand substantial rewards, as skilled researchers will prioritize platforms that offer competitive compensation. A well-structured payout system balances affordability for the organization with fair compensation for researchers, ensuring sustained interest and participation. Some companies also offer non-monetary incentives, such as job opportunities, security recognition, or leaderboard rankings, to attract and retain talent.

Bug bounty platforms contribute significantly to improving security awareness within organizations. Security teams gain insights into emerging attack techniques and common vulnerabilities, helping them implement proactive defenses. Development teams also benefit from exposure to real-world security issues, leading to better coding practices and stronger security integration in the software development lifecycle. Over time, continuous engagement with security researchers helps organizations build a more resilient security posture, reducing the likelihood of severe breaches.

While bug bounty programs are an effective security measure, they should not replace traditional security assessments. Combining bug bounty testing with internal security audits, code reviews, penetration testing, and automated scanning ensures comprehensive protection against a wide range of threats. Bug bounty programs work best as part of a layered security strategy, providing external validation of existing defenses while uncovering previously unknown risks.

Many organizations have successfully used bug bounty platforms to strengthen their security, including technology giants, financial institutions, and government agencies. These programs have uncovered critical vulnerabilities that could have led to data breaches, account takeovers, and infrastructure compromises. By fostering collaboration between ethical hackers and security teams, bug bounty platforms help organizations stay ahead of emerging threats and continuously improve their security posture.

Running an effective bug bounty program requires careful planning, clear guidelines, and a responsive security team. Organizations that embrace these platforms gain access to a vast community of skilled researchers, enhancing their ability to detect and mitigate vulnerabilities before they can be exploited. As cybersecurity threats continue to evolve, leveraging bug bounty platforms remains a proactive and cost-effective approach to securing modern web applications.

Building a Pentesting Lab

A penetration testing lab provides a controlled environment for security professionals and ethical hackers to test vulnerabilities, exploit security flaws, and refine their skills without affecting production systems. Constructing a well-designed lab is essential for learning attack techniques, developing defensive strategies, and conducting thorough security assessments. Whether used for personal learning, corporate security training, or research purposes, a pentesting lab must be carefully configured to simulate real-world attack scenarios while maintaining safety and isolation from external networks.

The foundation of a pentesting lab begins with selecting the appropriate hardware and software infrastructure. Many security professionals prefer virtualization technologies such as VMware, VirtualBox, or Proxmox to create isolated environments where multiple operating systems can run simultaneously. Virtualization allows testers to configure different network topologies, simulate enterprise environments, and quickly reset machines after conducting exploit tests. Dedicated hardware, such as a separate testing machine or a small-scale server, may be necessary for more advanced labs that require high performance or physical device interactions.

Choosing the right operating systems and target environments is crucial for a realistic pentesting lab. Common targets include intentionally vulnerable distributions such as Metasploitable, OWASP Broken Web Applications, and Damn Vulnerable Web Application (DVWA). These pre-configured environments contain known security flaws, making them ideal for learning attack techniques. Custom-built targets, including misconfigured servers, outdated applications, and insecure APIs, provide additional flexibility for testing specific vulnerabilities. A diverse set of targets ensures that security testers encounter a variety of security issues across different platforms and technologies.

Network segmentation is an important consideration when setting up a pentesting lab. Keeping the lab environment separate from production or personal networks prevents accidental attacks on real systems. Configuring a dedicated subnet, using virtual LANs (VLANs), or setting up a firewall to restrict external access helps maintain security and prevents unintentional data exposure. Some testers create an air-gapped environment, physically isolating the pentesting lab from the internet to eliminate risks associated with malware infections or unintended traffic leaks.

A complete pentesting lab includes a range of offensive security tools to simulate real-world attack scenarios. Tools such as Metasploit, Burp Suite, Nmap, and Wireshark provide essential capabilities for reconnaissance, exploitation, and network analysis. Custom scripts and exploit frameworks allow for deeper testing of vulnerabilities that may not be covered by off-the-shelf tools. Regular updates to testing tools and exploit databases ensure that the lab remains relevant to current security threats.

Simulating adversarial behavior requires configuring the lab to include realistic security controls and countermeasures. Setting up firewalls, intrusion detection systems, endpoint protection solutions, and logging mechanisms allows testers to evaluate how well defensive measures respond to attacks. Testing bypass techniques against security solutions provides valuable insights into their effectiveness and potential weaknesses. This approach helps both offensive and defensive teams understand how attackers evade detection and how security policies can be improved.

Automation and scripting play a significant role in pentesting labs, enabling testers to streamline common tasks, automate exploit execution, and simulate large-scale attacks. Scripting languages such as Python, PowerShell, and Bash allow for the creation of custom attack scenarios, log analysis tools, and automated report generation. Setting up a continuous testing environment using frameworks such as Ansible or Terraform allows for easy lab deployment, ensuring that environments can be reset and rebuilt efficiently after testing sessions.

Red teaming and adversary emulation scenarios enhance the effectiveness of a pentesting lab by simulating advanced threat actors. Setting up an internal Active Directory domain with misconfigurations, testing lateral movement techniques, and evaluating privilege escalation paths help security professionals understand complex attack chains. Running phishing simulations and social engineering tests within the lab environment provides additional insight into how attackers exploit human factors alongside technical vulnerabilities.

Expanding a pentesting lab to include cloud-based environments reflects modern security challenges. Configuring test instances on AWS, Azure, or Google Cloud allows testers to explore cloud security misconfigurations, identity and access management (IAM) weaknesses, and container security risks. Cloud environments introduce unique attack surfaces, such as serverless function exploitation, API abuse, and misconfigured storage buckets. A well-rounded lab includes both on-premises and cloud-based scenarios to ensure comprehensive security testing coverage.

Maintaining and improving a pentesting lab requires continuous updates, new challenge scenarios, and regular practice. As attack techniques evolve, security professionals must stay ahead by testing the latest exploits, studying emerging threats, and refining their methodologies. Incorporating real-world vulnerabilities discovered in recent security breaches into lab exercises ensures that testing remains relevant to modern attack techniques. Active participation in security communities, sharing findings, and engaging in capture-the-flag (CTF) competitions further enhance practical skills and knowledge.

A pentesting lab serves as a critical resource for developing offensive and defensive security expertise. By carefully designing an environment that includes diverse targets, realistic attack scenarios, and modern security tools, security professionals can improve their technical skills and stay prepared for evolving cyber threats. Investing in continuous learning, automation, and real-world testing methodologies ensures that a pentesting lab remains an effective training ground for ethical hacking and cybersecurity research.

Performing Red Team Simulations

Red team simulations are an essential component of modern cybersecurity strategies, allowing organizations to assess their defenses against real-world attack scenarios. Unlike traditional penetration testing, which focuses on identifying vulnerabilities in systems and applications, red teaming involves simulating advanced adversaries who attempt to breach an organization's security through various means. These simulations test not only technical security controls but also the effectiveness of incident response teams, detection mechanisms, and overall security resilience. By emulating real attackers, red teams help organizations uncover weaknesses that may not be detected through conventional testing methods.

A successful red team engagement begins with extensive reconnaissance, where attackers gather intelligence about the target organization. This phase involves mapping out infrastructure, identifying potential entry points, and researching employee behavior through open-source intelligence. Publicly available information, such as employee social media profiles, job postings, and leaked credentials, can provide valuable insights into an organization's security posture. Attackers use this information to craft tailored attack strategies that mimic the tactics, techniques, and procedures of real-world threat actors.

Social engineering plays a critical role in red team simulations, as human error remains one of the most significant security vulnerabilities. Attackers use phishing emails, phone-based impersonation, and physical intrusion techniques to bypass security controls. A well-crafted phishing campaign can trick employees into revealing credentials, installing malicious software, or granting unauthorized access to sensitive systems. By testing an organization's ability to detect and respond to social engineering attempts, red teams provide valuable insights into employee security awareness and the effectiveness of security training programs.

Once initial access is gained, red teams focus on maintaining persistence within the target environment. This involves using stealth techniques to evade detection while escalating privileges and laterally moving across the network. Attackers may exploit misconfigured security settings, weak authentication mechanisms, or outdated software to expand their access. Privilege escalation techniques, such as exploiting vulnerabilities in administrative tools or misconfigured permissions, allow attackers to move from an initial foothold to full domain compromise.

Evasion techniques are a crucial aspect of red teaming, as modern security defenses rely on endpoint detection, behavioral analysis, and intrusion detection systems to identify malicious activity. Attackers use custom malware, fileless attacks, and encrypted command-and-control channels to avoid triggering security alerts. By analyzing how well an organization detects and responds to stealthy threats, red teams help improve defensive strategies and refine incident response playbooks. Organizations that struggle to detect simulated adversaries may need to invest in better threat-hunting capabilities and behavioral analytics tools.

Data exfiltration is often the final objective of a red team simulation, testing an organization's ability to prevent unauthorized access to sensitive information. Attackers attempt to extract intellectual property, financial records, or customer data without being detected. Exfiltration methods include encrypting data before transmission, embedding stolen information in seemingly legitimate traffic, or leveraging cloud services to transfer data unnoticed. Security teams must analyze traffic patterns, implement anomaly detection, and enforce strict data access policies to mitigate the risks associated with data breaches.

After completing a red team engagement, a detailed debriefing process provides the organization with actionable insights into security gaps and areas for improvement. Red teams work closely with blue teams to review attack paths, discuss detection failures, and recommend mitigation strategies. Collaborative debriefings help security teams strengthen defenses, improve incident response workflows, and enhance their ability to detect and contain real-world threats. Regular red team simulations ensure that organizations remain proactive in addressing emerging threats and continuously improving their security posture.

Red team simulations serve as a critical tool for evaluating an organization's resilience against sophisticated cyber threats. By testing technical controls, employee awareness, and incident response capabilities, these exercises provide a realistic assessment of security readiness. Organizations that invest in regular red team assessments gain valuable insights into their vulnerabilities and develop a more robust defense strategy. The ability to detect, contain, and respond to simulated attacks ensures that security teams are prepared for real-world adversaries, reducing the likelihood of successful breaches and minimizing the impact of cyber incidents.

Web Application Security Standards and Frameworks

Web application security standards and frameworks provide organizations with structured guidelines to protect applications from cyber threats. As web applications continue to evolve, they become prime targets for attackers seeking to exploit vulnerabilities in authentication mechanisms, data storage, and communication protocols. Security standards serve as a foundation for secure development, helping organizations implement best practices, comply with regulatory requirements, and improve overall resilience against cyber threats.

One of the most widely recognized security frameworks for web applications is the Open Web Application Security Project (OWASP). OWASP maintains the OWASP Top Ten, a list of the most critical security risks affecting web applications. This document serves as a baseline for developers, security professionals, and auditors, highlighting vulnerabilities such as SQL injection, cross-site scripting (XSS), and security misconfigurations. OWASP also provides security testing guides, cheat sheets, and training resources that help organizations integrate security into the development lifecycle. By following OWASP recommendations, developers can proactively mitigate the most common attack vectors before they become exploitable.

The National Institute of Standards and Technology (NIST) also provides guidelines for securing web applications. The NIST Cybersecurity Framework offers a structured approach to identifying, protecting, detecting, responding to, and recovering from security incidents. While it is a general cybersecurity framework, it includes specific recommendations for web applications, such as encryption standards, access controls, and logging mechanisms. Organizations that adhere to NIST guidelines benefit from improved security postures, regulatory compliance, and better incident response capabilities.

The Payment Card Industry Data Security Standard (PCI DSS) is another critical framework that applies to web applications handling payment transactions. PCI DSS establishes strict security requirements for protecting credit card data, including encryption standards, secure authentication mechanisms, and logging requirements. Web applications that process payments must comply with PCI DSS to avoid financial penalties and reduce the risk of data breaches. Regular security assessments, vulnerability scanning, and penetration testing are required to maintain compliance with this standard.

The ISO/IEC 27001 standard provides a comprehensive information security management framework, covering web application security as part of a broader security strategy. It emphasizes risk management, access controls, and continuous security monitoring. Organizations that achieve ISO 27001 certification demonstrate a commitment to securing their web applications and protecting sensitive data. The standard requires regular security audits and risk assessments to ensure ongoing compliance and improvement.

Security frameworks such as the Center for Internet Security (CIS) Controls offer additional guidance on securing web applications. CIS provides a prioritized set of actions to defend against cyber threats, including secure software development practices, proper access control configurations, and continuous vulnerability management. By implementing CIS Controls, organizations can strengthen their security defenses and minimize the risk of exploitation.

Modern web applications increasingly rely on cloud environments, making cloud security frameworks essential. The Cloud Security Alliance (CSA) Cloud Controls Matrix provides guidelines for securing cloud-hosted applications, including identity and access management, data protection, and secure API usage. Organizations leveraging cloud-based web applications must ensure that security controls align with cloud security best practices to mitigate risks associated with cloud misconfigurations and unauthorized access.

Secure software development frameworks, such as Microsoft's Security Development Lifecycle (SDL) and Google's Web Security Guidelines, integrate security throughout the development process. These frameworks encourage threat modeling, secure coding practices, and automated security testing to reduce vulnerabilities in web applications. By incorporating security from the initial design phase, organizations can prevent security flaws from being introduced into production environments.

Web application security standards and frameworks serve as essential tools for organizations looking to secure their applications against evolving threats. By adhering to these guidelines, organizations can establish strong security controls, improve regulatory compliance, and reduce the likelihood of successful cyber attacks. Security teams, developers, and auditors must continuously update their security practices to align with industry standards, ensuring that web applications remain resilient in an ever-changing threat landscape.

Secure Development Lifecycle and Pentesting

The Secure Development Lifecycle (SDL) is a structured approach to integrating security into every phase of software development. It ensures that security considerations are addressed from the initial design phase through deployment and maintenance. By incorporating security practices early in the development process, organizations reduce the risk of vulnerabilities, minimize costly fixes, and improve overall application resilience. Penetration testing plays a crucial role in validating security measures, identifying weaknesses, and ensuring that software meets industry standards for secure coding and risk management.

A well-defined SDL begins with security requirements gathering, where development teams analyze potential threats and establish guidelines to mitigate them. Understanding the security landscape before writing code helps teams anticipate risks, define compliance objectives, and ensure that security measures align with business goals. Threat modeling techniques allow developers and security professionals to visualize attack scenarios, identify potential weak points, and implement proactive defenses. By addressing security at this early stage, organizations create a foundation for secure coding practices that extend throughout the development lifecycle.

The design phase of SDL incorporates architectural reviews and security assessments to ensure that applications are built with security in mind. Secure design principles, such as least privilege, defense-in-depth, and secure data handling, are applied to minimize attack surfaces. Developers evaluate authentication mechanisms, encryption standards, and access controls to reduce potential vulnerabilities. Reviewing third-party components and dependencies also prevents security risks associated with open-source libraries or external integrations. Architectural reviews ensure that security measures are embedded at the structural level, preventing design flaws that could be exploited later.

During the development phase, secure coding practices play a central role in reducing vulnerabilities. Developers follow secure coding guidelines, use static analysis tools to detect common flaws, and implement input validation to prevent injection attacks. Code reviews, conducted by peers or automated security tools, help identify security gaps before they make it into production. Secure coding frameworks, such as OWASP's secure coding principles, provide best practices for handling authentication, authorization, and data protection. By enforcing secure coding standards, development teams reduce the likelihood of introducing security weaknesses into the codebase.

Testing and validation are essential steps in SDL, ensuring that security controls function as intended. Automated security testing, including static application security testing (SAST) and dynamic application security testing (DAST), identifies vulnerabilities in both source code and runtime environments. Interactive application security testing (IAST) combines both approaches to provide real-time analysis during application execution. Security testing frameworks integrate with continuous integration pipelines to detect vulnerabilities early, allowing teams to address issues before they reach production.

Penetration testing serves as a critical component of the validation process, providing an external assessment of an application's security posture. Unlike automated security testing, pentesting involves skilled ethical hackers who simulate real-world attacks to uncover hidden vulnerabilities. Testers attempt to bypass authentication controls, exploit misconfigurations, and gain unauthorized access to sensitive data. Red teaming exercises extend pentesting by evaluating an organization's entire security ecosystem, including human factors, network infrastructure, and incident response capabilities. By conducting regular pentesting engagements, organizations gain valuable insights into their security weaknesses and improve their defenses accordingly.

The deployment phase of SDL includes security hardening techniques to protect applications from threats in production environments. Configuration management ensures that default settings are replaced with secure configurations, reducing exposure to common attacks. Logging and monitoring tools provide visibility into security events, enabling organizations to detect and respond to threats in real-time. Secure deployment pipelines enforce access controls, validate software integrity, and prevent unauthorized modifications. By integrating security into deployment workflows, organizations establish strong defenses against both internal and external threats.

Maintaining security after deployment requires continuous monitoring, vulnerability management, and patching strategies. Security teams track emerging threats, conduct regular security assessments, and apply patches to mitigate newly discovered vulnerabilities. Threat intelligence feeds provide insights into evolving attack patterns, allowing organizations to proactively defend against threats. Security incident response plans outline procedures for detecting, containing, and mitigating breaches, ensuring that organizations can respond effectively to security incidents. Ongoing security awareness training reinforces best practices among development and IT teams, strengthening an organization's overall security culture.

By integrating penetration testing into the Secure Development Lifecycle, organizations create a proactive approach to security that prevents vulnerabilities rather than reacting to them after deployment. SDL ensures that security is not treated as an afterthought but rather as a fundamental aspect of software development. Combining automated security testing, manual pentesting, and continuous monitoring enables organizations to build resilient applications that withstand evolving threats. A robust SDL framework enhances software security while maintaining agility, enabling organizations to innovate while protecting user data, business assets, and critical systems.

Continuous Integration and Continuous Deployment (CI/CD) Security

The adoption of Continuous Integration and Continuous Deployment (CI/CD) has transformed software development by enabling faster release cycles, automation of testing, and streamlined deployment processes. However, as CI/CD pipelines become more complex and integral to software development, they also introduce new security risks that attackers can exploit. Ensuring security at every stage of the CI/CD pipeline is critical to protecting source code, deployment environments, and production applications from potential breaches.

One of the key risks in CI/CD security is the exposure of sensitive credentials and secrets. Many organizations rely on environment variables, API keys, and authentication tokens to automate deployment processes. If these secrets are not properly managed, they can be leaked through misconfigured repositories, pipeline logs, or compromised build servers. Attackers who gain access to these credentials can manipulate build processes, deploy malicious code, or gain unauthorized entry into production environments. Implementing secret management solutions, encrypting sensitive information, and using access controls to limit exposure help mitigate this risk.

Another significant security concern is the integrity of source code within CI/CD pipelines. Attackers who gain unauthorized access to a version control system can inject malicious code that propagates through automated builds and deployments. This type of supply chain attack can introduce backdoors, alter application behavior, or compromise user data. Protecting source code requires enforcing strict access controls, enabling multi-factor authentication, and implementing branch protection rules to prevent unauthorized code modifications. Code reviews, digital signatures, and automated security scans further ensure that only trusted changes are deployed.

Third-party dependencies introduce another layer of risk in CI/CD environments. Many modern applications rely on open-source libraries and external dependencies that are integrated into builds through package managers. If these dependencies contain vulnerabilities or have been compromised, they can introduce security weaknesses into the final application. Attackers have exploited this vector in high-profile supply chain attacks, where malicious code was injected into widely used libraries. Regular dependency scanning, software composition analysis, and strict version control help mitigate the risk of incorporating vulnerable third-party components.

CI/CD pipelines also require secure build environments to prevent unauthorized modifications during the build process. Build servers often have elevated privileges and access to critical infrastructure, making them a prime target for attackers. If an attacker gains control over a build agent, they can inject malicious artifacts, modify configurations, or steal sensitive data. Isolating build environments, using ephemeral build agents, and enforcing least privilege access controls reduce the risk of build server compromise. Regular monitoring and logging of build activities provide additional visibility into potential security incidents.

Deployment security is another critical aspect of CI/CD pipeline protection. Automated deployment processes can be exploited if they do not verify the authenticity of deployed artifacts. Attackers can intercept deployment pipelines, replacing legitimate application components with malicious ones. Implementing cryptographic signing of artifacts, validating checksums, and enforcing strict deployment policies ensure that only verified and trusted code reaches production. Security teams should also monitor for unauthorized deployment attempts and enforce rollback procedures to mitigate potential incidents.

Another common attack vector in CI/CD environments is the abuse of misconfigured infrastructure as code (IaC) templates. Organizations often use tools such as Terraform, Ansible, or Kubernetes configurations to define and deploy infrastructure automatically. If these templates contain insecure configurations, such as excessive permissions, unprotected storage buckets, or publicly exposed services, they can introduce critical security risks. Automated security scanning of infrastructure configurations, enforcement of least privilege policies, and continuous compliance checks help reduce misconfigurations and prevent unintended exposure.

Security testing must be integrated into the CI/CD pipeline to identify vulnerabilities early in the development process. Traditional security assessments often occur too late in the software lifecycle, making it costly and time-consuming to remediate issues. Implementing automated security scans, static code analysis, and dynamic application security testing (DAST) within CI/CD workflows helps detect security flaws before deployment. Additionally, container security scanning ensures that containerized applications do not contain vulnerabilities or misconfigurations that could be exploited in production environments.

Monitoring and auditing are essential for maintaining the security of CI/CD environments. Security teams must have visibility into every stage of the pipeline, tracking code changes, build processes, and deployment activities. Logging mechanisms should capture detailed information on authentication events, access requests, and build modifications. Implementing anomaly detection and alerting systems allows organizations to detect suspicious activities and respond to security incidents in real time. Regular security audits help identify gaps in CI/CD security policies and ensure compliance with industry best practices.

Organizations must also establish clear security policies for development teams working within CI/CD environments. Security awareness training, secure coding practices, and role-based access controls help enforce a security-first mindset among developers. Establishing a culture of shared security responsibility ensures that security is integrated into development workflows rather than treated as an afterthought. By embedding security into the CI/CD pipeline, organizations can minimize risks while maintaining the speed and efficiency of modern software development practices.

Industry Trends in Web Application Pentesting

Web application penetration testing continues to evolve as cyber threats become more sophisticated and organizations increasingly rely on digital platforms. Security teams and ethical hackers must adapt to new attack techniques, emerging vulnerabilities, and changes in software development methodologies. The growing complexity of modern applications, the widespread adoption of cloud services, and the rise of artificial intelligence in cybersecurity are shaping the way pentesting is conducted. As regulatory requirements tighten and cybercriminals refine their methods, staying ahead of industry trends is critical for maintaining robust security defenses.

One of the most significant trends in web application pentesting is the shift toward continuous security testing. Traditional penetration testing was often performed as a one-time engagement, usually before a product launch or as part of an annual security assessment. However, with the rapid deployment cycles of modern web applications, vulnerabilities can emerge at any time. Organizations are increasingly adopting continuous security testing models, integrating automated scanning tools and frequent manual assessments into their development pipelines. Security testing is no longer a periodic event but an ongoing process designed to catch vulnerabilities before they reach production.

The rise of cloud-native applications has introduced new security challenges that pentesters must address. Web applications are no longer hosted on traditional infrastructure but are instead deployed across cloud platforms, containerized environments, and serverless architectures. Cloud security misconfigurations have become a leading cause of data breaches, making cloud-specific pentesting a necessity. Security testers now focus on identifying weaknesses in API gateways, misconfigured storage buckets, and identity and access management policies. The complexity of cloud environments requires pentesters to have expertise in cloud security frameworks and tools designed specifically for cloud-based penetration testing.

API security has become a central focus of modern pentesting efforts. With the proliferation of microservices and the increasing reliance on third-party integrations, APIs have become one of the primary attack vectors for web applications. API vulnerabilities, such as improper authentication, excessive data exposure, and broken access controls, have been responsible for major breaches in recent years. Organizations are placing greater emphasis on API security testing, requiring pentesters to assess API endpoints, validate authorization mechanisms, and ensure that sensitive data is not inadvertently exposed. API security testing tools and methodologies have advanced significantly, with techniques such as automated fuzzing, schema validation, and deep request manipulation becoming standard practices.

The role of artificial intelligence and machine learning in pentesting is another emerging trend. AI-driven security tools are being developed to assist with vulnerability detection, automate reconnaissance, and enhance attack simulation capabilities. While AI is not replacing human testers, it is improving efficiency by identifying patterns in large datasets and helping prioritize security risks. Machine learning models are also being used to analyze behavioral anomalies and detect potential threats that traditional security tools may overlook. Ethical hackers are exploring ways to leverage AI to conduct more thorough penetration tests, while organizations are using AI to enhance their defensive capabilities.

The growing importance of regulatory compliance and security frameworks has influenced the way web application pentesting is conducted. Many industries are now required to perform regular security assessments to comply with regulations such as GDPR, PCI DSS, HIPAA, and ISO 27001. These compliance requirements often dictate the scope and methodology of penetration tests, ensuring that organizations adhere to industry best practices. As regulatory bodies introduce stricter security guidelines, organizations must ensure that their security testing strategies align with these evolving compliance standards.

Bug bounty programs have also transformed the pentesting landscape by allowing companies to engage with a global community of ethical hackers. Instead of relying solely on internal security teams or external consultants, organizations are leveraging bug bounty platforms to identify vulnerabilities in real-time. Security researchers are incentivized to discover and report vulnerabilities before malicious actors can exploit them. This crowdsourced approach has proven effective in uncovering security flaws that traditional pentesting may miss. As a result, many organizations are combining structured pentesting with bug bounty programs to achieve a more comprehensive security assessment.

Red teaming engagements have gained popularity as organizations seek to test their security posture against real-world adversary techniques. Unlike standard pentests, which focus primarily on identifying vulnerabilities, red team exercises simulate targeted attacks against an organization's defenses. These simulations assess how well security teams detect, respond to, and mitigate actual attack scenarios. Red teaming incorporates social engineering, physical security assessments, and advanced attack techniques to provide a more realistic evaluation of an organization's security resilience. The demand for skilled red teamers has increased, driving the need for specialized training and certifications in offensive security methodologies.

As web applications become more complex, the use of DevSecOps practices is reshaping how security testing is integrated into the software development lifecycle. Security is no longer treated as a final step before deployment but is embedded throughout the development process. Automated security testing tools are being incorporated into CI/CD pipelines, allowing developers to identify and remediate vulnerabilities early in the development cycle. Pentesters are adapting to this shift by working more closely with development teams, helping implement security controls that prevent vulnerabilities from being introduced in the first place.

The increasing use of zero-trust security models is also influencing pentesting strategies. Traditional security models relied on perimeter defenses, but modern organizations are adopting zero-trust architectures that require continuous verification of users and devices. This shift requires pentesters to assess identity and access management policies, multi-factor authentication implementations, and endpoint security controls. By simulating attacks against zero-trust environments, security teams can validate whether these security models are effectively preventing unauthorized access.

Web application pentesting continues to evolve in response to new technologies, emerging threats, and shifting security priorities. As organizations embrace cloud computing, API-driven architectures, and AI-enhanced security tools, pentesters must adapt their methodologies to address these changes. The integration of continuous security testing, regulatory compliance requirements, bug bounty programs, and red teaming exercises ensures that security assessments remain effective against modern attack techniques. Keeping up with industry trends is essential for security professionals to stay ahead of adversaries and protect web applications from evolving cyber threats.

Emerging Technologies and Their Vulnerabilities

The rapid evolution of technology brings both advancements and new security challenges. As emerging technologies reshape industries, they introduce vulnerabilities that attackers can exploit. The increased adoption of artificial intelligence, blockchain, the Internet of Things, quantum computing, and 5G networks has led to a shift in attack surfaces, requiring new approaches to security. Organizations must anticipate these evolving threats and integrate security measures into the development and deployment of emerging technologies to reduce the risk of exploitation.

Artificial intelligence and machine learning are increasingly integrated into web applications, business processes, and cybersecurity defenses. While AI-powered security solutions help detect and mitigate threats, adversarial machine learning techniques allow attackers to manipulate AI models. Attackers can poison training datasets, causing AI models to produce inaccurate or biased results. Manipulating AI-generated responses in chatbots or fraud detection systems can lead to misinformation or unauthorized transactions. Additionally, AI automation in cybersecurity tools can be exploited if attackers manipulate input data to bypass detection. Organizations relying on

AI-driven solutions must implement mechanisms to verify data integrity and monitor for signs of adversarial attacks.

Blockchain technology promises secure, decentralized transactions, yet it is not immune to security risks. Smart contract vulnerabilities present one of the biggest threats in blockchain applications. Poorly coded smart contracts can be exploited through reentrancy attacks, integer overflows, or unauthorized function calls. Attackers have successfully drained millions of dollars from decentralized finance platforms by exploiting such flaws. Blockchain networks also face risks from 51% attacks, where attackers gain control of the network's mining or validation process, allowing them to manipulate transactions. While blockchain provides cryptographic security, weaknesses in implementation, key management, and consensus mechanisms can still be exploited.

The expansion of the Internet of Things has created a growing attack surface as billions of connected devices handle sensitive data and control critical infrastructure. Many IoT devices suffer from weak authentication, outdated firmware, and insecure communication channels. Attackers exploit these vulnerabilities to gain access to home automation systems, medical devices, industrial control systems, and smart city infrastructure. The lack of standardized security frameworks for IoT devices has resulted in inconsistent security practices across manufacturers. Compromised IoT devices can be used for large-scale botnet attacks, as seen in the case of Mirai, which exploited weak default credentials to launch massive distributed denial-of-service attacks.

Quantum computing poses both opportunities and threats to cybersecurity. While quantum processors offer unprecedented computational power, they also have the potential to break traditional encryption algorithms. Public key cryptography, which secures online transactions, VPN connections, and digital certificates, relies on mathematical problems that quantum computers could solve exponentially faster than classical computers. A sufficiently powerful quantum computer could render current encryption methods obsolete, exposing sensitive data to decryption. Cryptographers are working on quantum-resistant encryption algorithms, but organizations must prepare for the long-term impact of quantum advancements on existing security protocols.

The deployment of 5G networks introduces security concerns due to the increased number of connected devices, virtualization of network functions, and the reliance on software-defined infrastructure. The expanded attack surface in 5G environments makes it more challenging to detect and mitigate threats. Network slicing, which allows service providers to allocate network resources dynamically, could be exploited if access controls are not properly enforced. Supply chain security in 5G hardware and software components also raises concerns, as vulnerabilities in network infrastructure could be introduced at the manufacturing or deployment stages. As organizations adopt 5G technology, they must address risks related to data privacy, infrastructure integrity, and secure communication protocols.

As organizations integrate emerging technologies into their operations, the risk of cyberattacks targeting these advancements grows. Many new technologies are deployed before security risks are fully understood, leaving gaps that attackers can exploit. Security must be embedded at every stage of innovation, from research and development to deployment and maintenance. Organizations must adopt proactive security strategies, conduct thorough risk assessments, and implement security best practices tailored to the unique challenges of emerging technologies. By staying ahead of evolving threats, businesses and individuals can leverage technological advancements while minimizing the risks associated with their adoption.

Pentesting Progressive Web Apps (PWAs)

Progressive Web Apps (PWAs) have gained popularity as they combine the best features of traditional web applications and native mobile apps. PWAs offer improved performance, offline capabilities, push notifications, and a more engaging user experience without requiring installation from an app store. While these features provide significant advantages, they also introduce unique security challenges that must be considered during penetration testing. Ensuring that PWAs remain secure requires a thorough assessment of their architecture, storage mechanisms, network communication, and access control mechanisms.

A key aspect of PWA security testing involves analyzing how the application handles service workers. These scripts run in the background and enable offline functionality, caching strategies, and background synchronization. Service workers operate independently of the main web page, meaning they have access to a range of browser APIs, including fetch and push notifications. If not properly secured, attackers can exploit vulnerabilities in service workers to intercept network requests, manipulate cached content, or inject malicious scripts. A comprehensive pentest examines how service workers interact with network requests, ensuring that they are correctly scoped and do not expose sensitive data.

The application cache is another critical area of concern in PWA security. PWAs leverage caching mechanisms to enhance performance and enable offline access. However, improper caching configurations can lead to security risks, such as exposing sensitive information to unauthorized users or serving outdated and vulnerable application versions. Testing involves verifying that cache storage policies enforce proper access controls, ensuring that authentication tokens, user-specific data, and sensitive endpoints are not stored insecurely. Additionally, caching policies must be configured to prevent attackers from modifying stored content or injecting malicious payloads into cached resources.

PWAs rely heavily on HTTPS to ensure secure communication between the client and server. Unlike traditional web applications, PWAs often request permission for additional browser functionalities, such as geolocation, camera access, and push notifications. These permissions, if not properly managed, can be exploited by attackers to gain access to sensitive user data. Pentesters evaluate how PWAs request and enforce permissions, ensuring that excessive privileges are not granted unnecessarily. Additionally, testing includes verifying that permission requests follow best practices, such as prompting users only when necessary and properly handling permission revocations.

Cross-origin resource sharing (CORS) configurations are another crucial element in PWA security. Since PWAs interact with APIs to retrieve and update data, misconfigured CORS policies can expose them to cross-site scripting (XSS) and cross-site request forgery (CSRF) attacks. Pentesters analyze API request handling, ensuring that only trusted origins are allowed to access sensitive endpoints. Secure authentication and authorization mechanisms must be enforced to prevent unauthorized API access. API testing also includes evaluating how session tokens and credentials are transmitted, ensuring that they are protected against man-in-the-middle attacks and unauthorized interception.

Local storage mechanisms in PWAs introduce additional security considerations. Unlike traditional web applications that primarily rely on server-side storage, PWAs store significant amounts of data in the browser using IndexedDB, Web Storage, or Cache Storage. While these mechanisms improve performance and offline functionality, they can also become security risks if sensitive data is not properly encrypted or cleared when no longer needed. Attackers with access to the browser environment can extract stored data, manipulate session states, or execute injection attacks. Penetration testing includes assessing how PWAs store and handle sensitive information, ensuring that no authentication tokens, personally identifiable information, or critical business data remain exposed in client-side storage.

Authentication and session management in PWAs require careful evaluation. Since PWAs often function across multiple devices and network conditions, secure authentication mechanisms such as OAuth 2.0 and token-based authentication are commonly used. Testing focuses on verifying that authentication tokens are properly managed, ensuring that expired or revoked tokens cannot be reused. Multi-factor authentication and secure session timeout policies must also be enforced to prevent unauthorized access. Additionally, pentesters examine the implementation of biometric authentication or other alternative authentication methods commonly used in mobile-friendly applications.

Offline functionality testing is another essential component of pentesting PWAs. Since PWAs allow users to access certain features without an internet connection, attackers may exploit offline data synchronization mechanisms to manipulate transactions or inject malicious data. A thorough assessment evaluates how the application handles offline requests, ensuring that synchronization processes validate data integrity before committing changes to the server. Testing also includes simulating offline attack scenarios, such as modifying locally stored data and analyzing how the application reconciles these changes once connectivity is restored.

Ensuring that PWAs follow security best practices requires ongoing monitoring and updates. Since PWAs operate across multiple platforms and browsers, developers must stay informed about emerging vulnerabilities and implement security patches regularly. Pentesters assess whether the application enforces security headers, such as Content Security Policy (CSP), to mitigate XSS attacks and enforce safe script execution. Security headers, combined with proper sandboxing of third-party content, help reduce the risk of client-side attacks targeting PWA users.

Comprehensive penetration testing of PWAs ensures that security weaknesses are identified and mitigated before attackers can exploit them. By focusing on service worker security, caching policies, permissions management, secure storage, authentication mechanisms, and offline capabilities, organizations can protect their PWAs from emerging threats. A well-tested PWA not only provides a seamless user experience but also ensures that sensitive user data and application integrity remain secure across all usage scenarios.

Preparing for Web Application Pentesting Certifications

Earning a certification in web application penetration testing demonstrates expertise in identifying, exploiting, and mitigating security vulnerabilities in modern applications. As organizations prioritize cybersecurity, professionals with pentesting certifications gain recognition for their ability to assess application security effectively. Preparing for these certifications requires a combination of theoretical knowledge, hands-on practice, and a structured study approach to master the necessary skills. Many certification programs emphasize real-world scenarios, making practical experience just as important as understanding security concepts.

The first step in preparing for a web application pentesting certification is gaining foundational knowledge of web technologies, security principles, and attack methodologies. Web applications rely on protocols such as HTTP, authentication mechanisms, and session management techniques that must be thoroughly understood before attempting advanced security assessments. Understanding how web applications process user input, store data, and enforce access controls helps in identifying common weaknesses. Many certifications require familiarity with the OWASP Top Ten, which highlights the most prevalent security risks, including SQL injection, cross-site scripting, broken authentication, and security misconfigurations.

Hands-on experience is essential for success in pentesting certification exams. Many programs include practical labs that simulate real-world attack scenarios, requiring candidates to demonstrate their skills in live environments. Setting up a personal pentesting lab with vulnerable web applications allows candidates to practice techniques such as reconnaissance, exploitation, and privilege escalation. Open-source tools such as Burp Suite, OWASP ZAP, and SQLmap provide valuable experience in testing web applications for vulnerabilities. Platforms like Hack The Box, TryHackMe, and PortSwigger's Web Security Academy offer interactive challenges that help candidates refine their skills.

Understanding the methodology used in web application penetration testing is crucial when preparing for certification exams. A structured approach includes reconnaissance, enumeration, vulnerability identification, exploitation, and post-exploitation analysis. Certifications often evaluate a candidate's ability to follow a systematic testing process rather than relying solely on automated scanning tools. Developing strong documentation skills is also necessary, as many exams require candidates to submit reports detailing their findings, attack vectors, and recommended mitigations. Clear and structured reporting ensures that technical and non-technical audiences can understand the security risks identified during an assessment.

Certifications vary in difficulty and focus, with some emphasizing theoretical knowledge and others requiring hands-on assessments. The Offensive Security Web Expert (OSWE) certification, for example, focuses on white-box testing and requires candidates to analyze source code to identify vulnerabilities. The GIAC Web Application Penetration Tester (GWAPT) certification covers a broad range of web security topics, including authentication flaws, business logic vulnerabilities, and web services security. The Certified Ethical Hacker (CEH) certification provides a more general overview of ethical hacking techniques, including web application security. Understanding the objectives and structure of a certification exam helps candidates tailor their study plan accordingly.

Time management plays a critical role in preparing for pentesting certification exams, especially those with hands-on components. Some exams require candidates to complete practical assessments within a limited timeframe, making efficiency an important factor in success. Practicing under timed conditions helps candidates develop strategies for identifying vulnerabilities quickly, prioritizing attack paths, and documenting findings efficiently. Familiarity with command-line tools, scripting languages, and automation techniques further enhances a candidate's ability to complete assessments within the allotted time.

Many pentesting certifications require a strong understanding of exploit development and payload customization. While automated tools assist in vulnerability discovery, candidates must also be able to craft manual exploits and modify existing attack scripts to bypass security controls. Knowledge of programming languages such as Python, JavaScript, and Bash scripting can be advantageous when customizing attack payloads or automating repetitive testing tasks. Certifications that emphasize exploit development often require candidates to demonstrate creativity in bypassing security mechanisms rather than relying solely on known vulnerabilities.

Collaboration with the security community enhances the preparation process by providing access to study resources, mentorship, and real-world insights. Engaging with cybersecurity forums, attending security conferences, and participating in Capture The Flag (CTF) competitions help candidates stay updated on emerging attack techniques. Many certification providers offer online study groups, practice exams, and training courses that guide candidates through the certification process. Networking with experienced professionals and learning from their experiences provides valuable perspectives on common pitfalls and best practices.

Successfully obtaining a web application pentesting certification validates a candidate's ability to assess application security and identify vulnerabilities that could lead to data breaches or system compromise. The certification process requires dedication, persistence, and a commitment to continuous learning, as cybersecurity threats constantly evolve. By combining theoretical knowledge with hands-on practice, structured study plans, and real-world testing experience, candidates can develop the expertise necessary to pass certification exams and apply their skills in professional security assessments.

Ethical Considerations in Web Application Testing

Web application testing is a critical component of cybersecurity, helping organizations identify vulnerabilities before they can be exploited by malicious actors. Ethical considerations play a fundamental role in ensuring that testing is conducted responsibly, legally, and with respect for privacy. Security professionals must balance the need to uncover security flaws with the obligation to protect sensitive data and comply with legal and regulatory requirements. Without a strong ethical foundation, security testing can cross into unethical or even illegal territory, resulting in reputational damage and legal consequences.

One of the primary ethical concerns in web application testing is obtaining proper authorization. Testing without explicit permission is considered unauthorized access, which is illegal in many jurisdictions under computer fraud and cybercrime laws. Ethical hackers and penetration testers must ensure they have formal approval from the organization before conducting security assessments. This approval process often involves signing legal agreements that outline the scope, methodology, and rules of engagement to ensure that all testing activities are conducted within legal boundaries. Clear communication between security testers and stakeholders helps establish trust and prevents unintended consequences.

Respect for user privacy is another crucial aspect of ethical web application testing. Many web applications process personal and sensitive data, including financial records, medical information, and private communications. Security testers must take extra precautions to avoid exposing, modifying, or mishandling this data during testing. Ethical hackers should use test accounts and simulated data whenever possible to minimize the risk of compromising real user information. If personal data is encountered during testing, it must be handled with strict confidentiality and reported responsibly without unnecessary exposure. Organizations should also define clear guidelines on how security testers should interact with sensitive data to ensure compliance with privacy laws such as GDPR and HIPAA.

Responsible disclosure is a fundamental principle of ethical web application testing. When security vulnerabilities are identified, testers must follow a structured process for reporting issues to the organization in a way that allows them to be remediated before being disclosed publicly. Coordinated vulnerability disclosure programs provide a framework for researchers to report findings while giving companies the opportunity to fix security issues before they are exploited. Ethical hackers must resist the temptation to disclose vulnerabilities prematurely or use them for personal gain. In cases where an organization does not respond to a responsible disclosure attempt, researchers must carefully consider the potential impact of making vulnerability details public and follow established ethical guidelines for responsible reporting.

The potential for unintended damage is another ethical concern in web application testing. Security tests, especially those involving automated tools or aggressive attack simulations, can cause system disruptions, performance degradation, or data corruption if not conducted carefully. Ethical testers must ensure that their methods do not negatively impact system availability or user experience. Testing should be conducted in controlled environments whenever possible, and when live systems must be tested, safeguards should be in place to prevent unintended consequences. A well-defined testing plan that includes monitoring and rollback procedures helps mitigate the risk of accidental harm.

Ethical considerations extend to the intent and professionalism of security testers. A core principle of ethical hacking is to work in good faith, aiming to strengthen security rather than exploit weaknesses for personal or financial gain. Ethical testers must maintain integrity, avoiding conflicts of interest and adhering to professional codes of conduct established by organizations such as the EC-Council, Offensive Security, and other cybersecurity certification bodies. Security professionals should also commit to continuous education, staying updated on legal and ethical guidelines as the field evolves.

Web application security testing also raises ethical questions about third-party services and supply chain security. Many web applications rely on external vendors, APIs, and cloud services, which may introduce security vulnerabilities beyond the direct control of the organization being tested. Ethical testers must navigate these complexities carefully, ensuring that security assessments do not inadvertently violate agreements with third-party providers. When vulnerabilities are discovered in third-party components, disclosure must be handled with sensitivity to avoid exposing businesses to unnecessary risks while ensuring that security issues are addressed.

Cultural and legal differences across jurisdictions further complicate the ethical landscape of web application testing. Different countries have varying laws regarding cybersecurity practices, data protection, and hacking activities. What may be considered ethical and legal in one country could be prohibited in another. Security professionals working across international borders must familiarize themselves with local regulations and obtain necessary legal approvals before conducting tests. Ethical hackers engaged in bug bounty programs must also be aware of the specific rules and policies of each platform to avoid violating terms of service or inadvertently engaging in unauthorized activities.

Ethical web application testing requires a strong commitment to responsible practices, legal compliance, and professional integrity. Security professionals must prioritize authorization, respect user privacy, practice responsible disclosure, minimize unintended harm, and adhere to ethical standards in all testing activities. By following ethical principles, testers contribute to a safer internet while maintaining trust with organizations and users. The evolving nature of cybersecurity means that ethical considerations will continue to play a crucial role in shaping best practices for security testing and responsible vulnerability management.

Final Thoughts and Future of Web Application Pentesting

Web application penetration testing has evolved significantly as organizations increasingly rely on web-based services and cloud infrastructure. Cybersecurity threats continue to grow in complexity, and adversaries adapt their techniques to bypass traditional security controls. The role of penetration testers has expanded beyond simple vulnerability assessments to a continuous process that integrates security testing with development and operations. The need for proactive security strategies, automated tools, and human expertise is greater than ever as organizations face constant pressure to safeguard sensitive data and maintain regulatory compliance.

The shift toward automation in security testing has transformed the way web application pentesting is conducted. Traditional manual testing methods, while thorough, can be time-consuming and limited in scale. Automated vulnerability scanners and artificial intelligence-driven security solutions have accelerated the detection of common vulnerabilities, allowing security teams to focus on more complex attack vectors. Despite these advancements, human-driven testing remains essential, as automated tools cannot fully replicate the creativity and adaptability of a skilled ethical hacker. The future of pentesting will likely involve a hybrid approach that combines the efficiency of automation with the depth of manual testing.

The increasing use of cloud computing has introduced new challenges for web application security. Many modern applications are built using microservices, serverless architectures, and containerized environments that require specialized testing methodologies. Security professionals must adapt their testing strategies to assess API security, cloud misconfigurations, and identity management controls. Organizations are also adopting zero-trust security models, where trust is never assumed, and verification is required at every access point. Pentesters will need to evaluate how these security measures are implemented and whether they effectively prevent unauthorized access.

The adoption of DevSecOps has made security an integral part of the software development lifecycle. Security testing is no longer a standalone activity but a continuous process embedded into CI/CD pipelines. Developers are increasingly responsible for implementing secure coding practices, while security teams focus on detecting vulnerabilities earlier in the development cycle. This shift requires pentesters to collaborate more closely with development teams, providing guidance on secure coding and integrating security tools into automated workflows. The role of pentesters is evolving from external assessors to embedded security engineers who contribute to ongoing security improvements.

Threat actors continue to refine their techniques, making web applications an attractive target for cyberattacks. Sophisticated phishing campaigns, supply chain attacks, and zero-day exploits present new challenges that require security professionals to stay ahead of emerging threats. Bug bounty programs have played a significant role in uncovering vulnerabilities by leveraging the expertise of ethical hackers worldwide. Organizations are increasingly embracing crowdsourced security testing as a complement to traditional pentesting efforts, allowing for continuous security assessment from diverse perspectives.

Regulatory requirements and data protection laws are also shaping the future of web application pentesting. Compliance standards such as GDPR, PCI DSS, and ISO 27001 mandate regular security assessments and vulnerability management. Organizations must ensure that their security practices align with these evolving regulations, which often dictate the scope and frequency of penetration testing. As governments introduce stricter cybersecurity policies, pentesters will need to stay informed about legal and regulatory developments to ensure compliance while conducting security assessments.

The demand for skilled penetration testers continues to grow as businesses recognize the importance of proactive security testing. However, the industry faces a talent shortage, with organizations struggling to find qualified professionals who possess both technical expertise and a deep understanding of attack methodologies. Security training programs, certifications, and hands-on experience through platforms like Capture The Flag (CTF) competitions and bug bounty programs are helping bridge this skills gap. Future pentesters must continuously expand their knowledge, experiment with new attack techniques, and stay updated on evolving threats to remain effective in the field.

As cyber threats become more advanced, organizations must adopt a security-first mindset that prioritizes proactive defense strategies. The future of web application pentesting will require a blend of automation, human expertise, regulatory compliance, and continuous security integration. By staying ahead of emerging threats, adapting to technological changes, and fostering a culture of security awareness, businesses can enhance their resilience against cyberattacks while maintaining trust with users and stakeholders.